FORT WAYNE

CITY *of* SPIRIT

Entrance

INTRODUCTION BY KEITH EDWARDS ◆ ART DIRECTION BY BRIAN GROPPE

URBAN
TAPESTRY
SERIES
TOWERY
PUBLISHING, INC.

FORT WAYNE
CITY of SPIRIT

CONTENTS

FORT

WAYNE

By Keith Edwards

I left Colorado Springs in the summer of 1983, after working there a couple of years as a television news anchor. It was a great place, and I left there with the Garden of the Gods' red sandstone still in my shoes, and the breathtaking view of Pikes Peak from my living room still in my mind. However, you can't take the Midwest out of the boy, as they say, so I headed back. Not to my hometown of Grosse Pointe, Michigan, but to where midwestern living is at its best—to Fort Wayne, a shimmering, iridescent gem in the middle of an agricultural paradise.

When I first arrived here in 1983 to take a job at WPTA as a news anchor, everyone told me I would love it, that it was a great place to raise a family. They were right: Fort Wayne—which is known by many names, from the Summit City and Three Rivers City to the City of Churches and the All-American City—is, in fact, an excellent place to call home. The perks and amenities of big-city life are in abundance, but we also have easy access to the serenity and peacefulness of country living. Our location could not be better. We're about two hours from Indianapolis, three hours from Chicago and Detroit, and only a bit more than that to Cleveland and Cincinnati. It's no wonder, then, that more than 190,000 people live and work in Fort Wayne, making it Indiana's second-largest city. Nor is it surprising that *Money* magazine placed it at number 75 in its 1997 ranking of the best places to live in the United States.

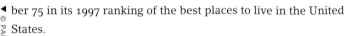

And why wouldn't we have such a high ranking? The housing here is unbelievably affordable, far below the national median, and the crime rate is impressively low. There are wonderful parks—87 of them—at practically every turn. We have an excellent array of sporting diversions, terrific schools and universities, and a top-notch arts community. And it must be an excellent place to do business, judging from the number of local, national, and international corporations and plants that have kept our industry humming—and the economy growing—since the 1800s. We have excellent highways and rail and air systems; Fort Wayne International Airport has a 12,000-foot runway and has undergone $29 million in improvements since 1996. The folks at the Greater Fort Wayne Chamber of Commerce call all of this "infrastructure and transportation." I like to think of it as just another component of the comfortable, stimulating environment that defines the appeal of Fort Wayne.

Certainly the environment in Fort Wayne has helped to motivate and encourage freethinkers, creative minds, and industrious innovators, from Wendy's hamburger king Dave Thomas to Philo T. Farnsworth and the other engineers at Magnavox who developed the technology for television. Both the electric refrigerator and the electric razor were developed here by the sharp minds at General Electric—in addition to the first garbage disposal, the first washing machine, handheld calculators, streetlights, gas pumps, and the technology that paved the way for the invention of the jukebox. You can also thank the Magnavox folks for introducing to the lexicon of audiophilia such terms as "woofer," "tweeter," and "stereophonic." Additionally, Fort Wayne is the birthplace of actresses Carole Lombard, Marilyn Maxwell, Julie Barr, and Shelley Long; soap star Drake Hogestyn; Dan Butler of TV's *Frasier*; NFL All-Pro cornerback Rod Woodson; Seattle Seahawks cornerback Joey Eloms; and world-renowned clothing designer Bill Blass, among others.

That's more than just a formidable list of some trailblazing accomplishments and luminaries from the fields of sports, entertainment, and fashion. There's something emblematic in that list—emblematic of the spirit of Fort Wayne, of what makes the place so special.

Fort Wayne was named after the revered General "Mad" Anthony Wayne. A decorated hero of the Revolutionary War, Wayne was sent into Miami Indian territory in 1794 and led two victorious battles in Ohio—at Fort Recovery and Fallen Timbers (an area that would later be renamed Toledo). He then moved his troops farther along the Maumee River near the village of Kekionga, at the confluence of

the Maumee, St. Joseph, and St. Mary's rivers. It was here that Wayne established the fort that would bear his name, located at what is now the intersection of Clay and Berry streets.

Establishing the fort was no easy task, as there were numerous skirmishes and outright battles with the Native Americans who had lived in the area since the early 1700s (and who were allied with the British through much of the Revolutionary War). Among the most legendary and combative Native American leaders in the region during the war was Chief Little Turtle of the Miami Indians, who waged numerous successful battles against American troops, most notably the 1790 Battle of Kekionga. As he grew older, though, Little Turtle came to favor negotiations with these new settlers. He took up causes to better the lives of Native Americans, from spearheading a campaign to keep white men from selling liquor to his people to participating in the signing of the Treaty of Greenville, which opened to settlement a strip of eastern Indiana and half of Ohio. Little Turtle died in 1812, a respected figure among whites and a respected leader among Native Americans. His grave is marked in Fort Wayne at a small memorial park on Lawton Place.

THE DIVERSITY OF FORT WAYNE'S CITIZENRY STRETCHES BACK TO THE EARLY 1800S, BY WHICH TIME the city had amassed a small population of various Native American tribes, American settlers, and French and American traders. It wasn't until 1832, however, when ground was broken for the Wabash and Erie Canal, that the area was transformed from an outback trading post to a cosmopolitan city, increasingly reliant

upon both industry and agriculture. Myriad construction projects brought a flux of workers to the area—including emigrants from Germany and Ireland—and by the mid-1800s, with the arrival of the railroads, Fort Wayne had grown to become one of Indiana's largest cities.

Despite the constant growth and continued technological advances that have made Fort Wayne a thoroughly modern metropolis for more than a century, we have always cherished our history. And with our many museums, exhibits, monuments, and festivals, we proudly celebrate Fort Wayne's legacy and the people who have contributed to it.

Among the most famous by far is John Chapman, an American folk hero better known as Johnny Appleseed. Chapman traveled the countryside on foot through the early 1800s, from his home state of Pennsylvania to Ohio and Indiana; planting apple tree seedlings and caring for the sick and the elderly. In 1845, at the age of 71, he succumbed to the "winter plague" and was buried along the St. Joseph River. A commemorative marker stands on the hill in Archer Park—also known as Johnny Appleseed Park—where the Johnny Appleseed Festival is held in the famous planter's honor every September. The nonprofit affair offers a panoply of entertainment and diversions, from music and farmers markets to a Native American village, a spectacular fireworks display, and a loaded menu of delicacies cooked over open fires, 19th-century style. Chapman would have loved it.

Fort Wayne has ties to Abraham Lincoln, although they're sort of loose. Although the Lincoln family settled here in the early 1800s before eventually moving to Illinois, the Great Emancipator himself was in Fort Wayne only once, and that was to change trains. Yet, the world's largest private collection of Lincoln memorabilia available to the public is located here at the Lincoln Museum on East Berry Street. Its 11 galleries overflow with everything from portraits and letters to engravings and books. Touch-screen computer exhibits bring high-tech convenience to the museum, and its research library contains some 18,000 books and 5,000 original photographs.

Much of Fort Wayne's architecture has withstood the wrecker's ball of urban renewal—including the Lincoln National Bank and Trust Building (among the tallest in the state) and the gorgeous Embassy Centre, both from the late 1920s—which contributes to the city's old-style ambience. Fittingly, the Old City Hall Historical Museum offers visitors a chance to take a trip back in time and learn something during the journey. Housed in a century-old sandstone castle that was once Fort Wayne's city hall and jail, the museum features everything from a detailed model of a Native American village to an actual downtown storefront from the late 1800s, not to mention loads of interesting trivia. (For instance, the old copper-made Christmas tree tinsel was manufactured in Fort Wayne at such companies as the Essex Corporation and Rea Magnet Wire.)

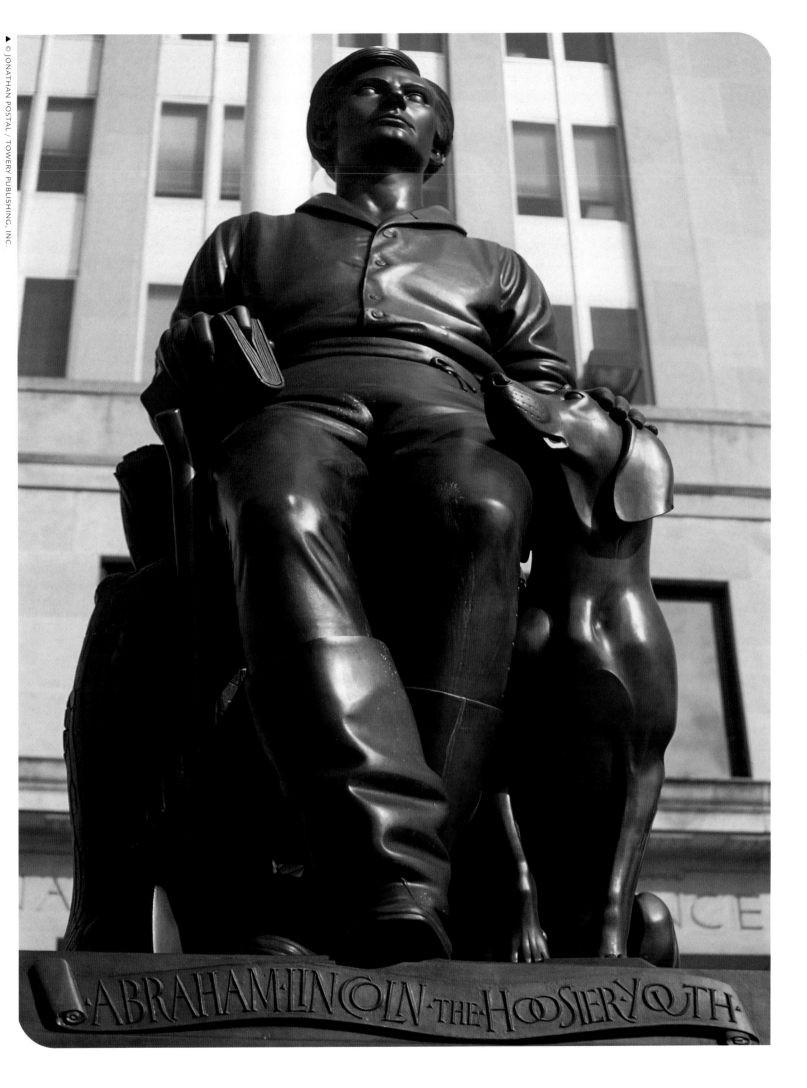

ABRAHAM·LINCOLN·THE·HOOSIER·YOUTH·

The Firefighters' Museum on West Washington Boulevard is a monument to our city's firemen, located in the old Engine House No. 3, which was built in 1893 and expanded in 1907 and 1909 until it became Fort Wayne's largest firehouse. Although today it is primarily an educational resource, with information and classes on fire safety (including the ever popular fire safety maze), the museum features a reconstructed version of the original firehouse, which gives you an idea of what it was like for the six men who manned the old brick station back in the late 1800s. And over on O'Day Road, we have Veterans Memorial Park, a sobering place for the remembrance and honoring of those who gave the ultimate sacrifice in service to this country.

Through these monuments and exhibits, it is obvious that Fort Waynians have learned that the road to the future leads to nowhere if you forget—or take for granted—the efforts of those who helped to pave that road.

To say that Fort Wayne is a city obsessed with sports would be like saying Indiana Pacers guard Reggie Miller is a pretty good basketball player. We're nuts about it, from high school football to minor-league baseball. And Hoosier basketball tops the list of our collective obsession. Practically every house in the city has a basketball goal affixed above the driveway, and the sports-loving masses rally around both the Indianapolis-based Pacers and the Fort Wayne Fury, the 1996 American Conference champions of the Continental Basketball Association. (An interesting basketball footnote: Fort Wayne is the original home of the Zollner Pistons, which later moved to Detroit and became the Pistons of the NBA.)

© JONATHAN POSTAL / TOWERY PUBLISHING, INC.

The Fury shares its home turf at the Allen County War Memorial Coliseum and Memorial Stadium with the Komets, Fort Wayne's team in the United Hockey League and winners of the 1993 Turner Cup. It's also the place where our Class-A Wizards take to the baseball field each summer. The Midwest League team is affiliated with the San Diego Padres.

Speaking of baseball, Fort Wayne had the distinction of hosting the first professional league baseball game—a May 4, 1871, match at Camp Allen Park between the Fort Wayne Kekiongas and the Cleveland Forest Citys, both in the National Association of Professional Baseball Players. Fittingly, the Kekiongas won. And more than a decade later, that same park was the site of the first baseball game played under lights. Although some historians dispute this claim, these facts remain: On June 22, 1883, the Quincy Professionals and players from the Fort Wayne Methodist College played on a field set aglow thanks to the Jenny Electric Light Company—a hometown company founded in the early 1880s—which provided 17 Jenny Arc Lamps of 4,000 candlepower each. Newspaper accounts claim that more than 2,000 spectators were on hand for the game, during which the lights went out at least twice. Quincy emerged victorious, beating our home team 19 to 11. Regardless of the loss, it must have been a real sight.

If you're a golf whiz, or just a duffer like me, Fort Wayne has more than 20 public courses and a variety of private clubs, among them the Jack Nicklaus-designed Sycamore Hills on the southwest side of town. It's a beautiful course, with homes to match. Other great places to play include Chestnut Hills (designed by links legend Fuzzy Zoeller), Cherry Hill, Autumn Ridge, Orchard Ridge, and Brookwood, to name a few.

And golf in Fort Wayne means more than just a (hopefully) relaxing day on a sun-bathed course. During the annual Mad Anthony's Celebrity Pro-Am, hosted by 280 business professionals, a group of PGA and LPGA pros, joined by other sports and entertainment celebrities, gather to play golf and earn money for local charities. More than $1.5 million has been raised since the Pro-Am was founded. There's also the Vera Bradley Classic, named after the famed, Fort Wayne-based handbag, clothing, and luggage company. This women's golf tournament has generated thousands of dollars, all donated for breast cancer research.

Churches played a vital role in the early development of Fort Wayne, and they continue to provide the spiritual backbone of the city and its people, with every denomination well represented among the more than 350 houses of worship. (Why do you think we're known as the City of Churches?) The city is also home to the Bishop of the Fort Wayne-South Bend Diocese of the Catholic Church, Bishop John D'Arcy, based at the Catholic Cathedral of the Immaculate Conception. An example of the population's passion and faith: In 1993, St. Mary's Catholic Church in downtown Fort Wayne was struck by lightning and burned to the ground. There were dramatic photos taken of the steeple tumbling to the ground in flames,

this century-old architectural marvel reduced to a massive pile of white-hot rubble. The congregation came together, however, and today a new St. Mary's sits at the same location and has continued to serve the community since its official reopening in October 1998.

Although Fort Wayne has managed to maintain its small-town charm and appeal through the years, the wheels of industry turn fast here. And the city has an abundance of educational opportunities, with more than 15 colleges and universities in the area. Chief among them is Indiana University-Purdue University, Fort Wayne, which boasts a nearly 600-acre campus and numbers more than 10,000 undergraduate and graduate students, while Indiana Vocational Technical College and the Indiana Institute of Technology are preparing their classes for the latest cutting-edge jobs.

And a number of those jobs can be found right here in the Summit City, the birthplace of many technological innovations via still-thriving companies such as ITT and magnet wire manufacturers such as Phelps Dodge, Essex, and Rea Magnet Wire. Major employers in the city also include General Motors and North American Van Lines, among many, many others. Oh, we also have an ice-cream plant responsible for the delicacies offered up by Edy's Grand Ice Cream, as well as those under the Ben & Jerry's banner.

As a television news anchor, I've done more than my share of traveling, and I've been to a slew of different cities of varying sizes. And I have to say, the Summit City is up there with the best in

© JONATHAN POSTAL / TOWERY PUBLISHING, INC.

more ways than I can count. Chief among them is Fort Wayne's thriving arts community, anchored by the Arts United of Greater Fort Wayne. Among the oldest and largest arts funders in the United States (it was established in 1955), the umbrella group helps manage and raise money for numerous galleries, museums, and exhibits, and boasts 53 member organizations, including film, dance, and historical groups.

The Fort Wayne Museum of Art has more than 1,300 works in its permanent collection, including scores of European and American paintings, drawings, and sculpture spanning the 19th and 20th centuries, and featuring the creations of many local and regional artists. The museum's roots stretch back to the late 1880s, when J. Ottis Adams, and later William Forsyth, taught informal drawing and painting classes; the current museum was opened in 1984, and features a gorgeous skylight that contributes greatly to the ambience of this nearly 40,000-square-foot Fort Wayne gem.

For vintage films, concerts, and Broadway shows and musicals, the Embassy Centre is the place. Included on the National Register of Historic Places, the Embassy was completed in 1928 and served as Fort Wayne's quintessentially majestic performance and movie palace until its screen darkened—for good, so it seemed—in the early 1970s. Fortunately, a volunteer group emerged to save the old brick- and terra-cotta-trimmed structure, and in 1980, it was restored to its original splendor. And yes, the Page Theatre Organ—one of only four ever made—is still there, in all its 1920s-era glory.

The Fort Wayne Philharmonic is led by the acclaimed maestro Edvard Tchivzhel. For 38 weeks each year, it presents terrific programs at the Performing Arts Center where, in addition to local and touring musicals and plays, you can also catch the top-notch Fort Wayne Ballet, an institution in the city's fine-arts community since 1956. Its annual staging of *The Nutcracker* has become a local Christmas tradition.

Another Fort Wayne tradition, and a summertime favorite for more than 30 years, is the Three Rivers Festival and its parade, which I have proudly cohosted since 1988. For a full week in early July, hundreds of thousands of people from across the region gather downtown—at Freimann Square and Headwaters Park—for a blowout of food, music, arts, and crafts. It's all kicked off with a glorious parade that includes as many as 150 entrants, and culminates with an explosive fireworks display. (And while you're there, treat yourself to an elephant ear—a big gob of lightly fried dough that's sprinkled liberally with cinnamon. Forget about the calories; it's a sweet indulgence.)

If you're looking for a place to have a picnic, take a walk, throw a Frisbee, hear some music, or just relax beneath the shade of a huge tree, Fort Wayne has plenty of spots for you. The sprawling, 22-acre grounds of Headwaters Park in downtown Fort Wayne offer an ideal setting for numerous festivals throughout the year, many of which salute the city's rich ethnic heritages, including Greek, German,

and African-American cultures. It's also a fine place for a wedding or a family reunion. And while you're downtown, be sure to stop in at the Foellinger-Freimann Botanical Conservatory, the Midwest's largest passive solar conservatory and one of the most popular attractions in the city, drawing up to 90,000 visitors annually. You'll find three totally unique green thumb experiences: the Tropical House, with exotic plants; the Arid House, with cacti and other flora; and the Showcase House, which features six seasonal displays each year. Our Lakeside Rose Garden, meanwhile, is one of the city's largest rose gardens, with more than 2,000 rose bushes. Naturally, it's a favorite location for weddings and picnics.

Among the other parks worth seeking out is Lawton Park, site of Kids Crossing, designed during the Bicentennial by local children and built by volunteers. And you have to see our nearly 15-mile stretch of beauty called Rivergreenway, which connects the city from one side to the other, and winds along the St. Joseph, Maumee, and St. Mary's rivers. It's the path of choice for countless cyclists, joggers, and walkers.

For science buffs of all ages, Science Central, located in the old city light and power plant—just look for the multicolored smokestacks—will not disappoint. Through hands-on exhibits, you can learn about everything from tornadoes and earthquakes to how the weather can be predicted. There are a slew of games and displays that, believe it or not, make mathematics seem fun; you can also make your own tornado, stick your face in a cloud, and defy gravity via a bicycle ride that takes you 20 feet off the ground. Another great learning experience for the kids can be found at the Fort Wayne Children's Zoo, visited by

more than 500,000 people each year and considered to be among the finest menageries in the United States. Its 42 acres contain everything from the Indonesian Rain Forest and the Orangutan Valley to the lavishly landscaped Tiger Valley and a massive herd of kangaroos.

TAKE A DRIVE THROUGH FORT WAYNE SOMETIME AND YOU'LL soon figure out why it's often referred to as the City of Restaurants: We have more than 400 eateries here, spanning the culinary gamut— from home-cooking diners to five-star bastions of gourmet finery; from French, Italian, and Asian to German, Russian, and Hispanic; from seafood and barbecue to steaks and Coney Island hot dogs. We would need a second book to catalog the best dining this city has to offer, from the regular haunts of Fort Wayne gourmands to those establishments that appreciate the art of the perfect cheeseburger.

A few epicurean institutions must be named, however, starting with the Oyster Bar, Fort Wayne's oldest restaurant-cum-tavern, the perfect place for oceanic victuals and spirits since it was established in 1888. The award-winning Café Johnell started its life back in the 1950s as a carryout pizzeria. For the last 40 years, though, it has earned a national and international reputation as one of the finest French restaurants in the world. Another long-time favorite is La Hacienda, a family-owned Mexican place where the food is as authentic as the Trevino clan's hospitality. The dogs at the Coney Island on downtown's Main Street have kept Fort Waynians happy since the 1940s, and the atmosphere retains its nostalgic charm, right down to the Coca-Colas served in those classic little bottles. And spring and summer in Fort Wayne would be unthinkable without stopping in for a cone or a sundae at Zesto's, a time-traveling experience that can always clear the head after a long day at the office or in the classroom.

Like our city's array of culinary choices—from the time-honored eateries to the latest places on the block—Fort Wayne offers its residents and its visitors a vast collection of diversions and opportunities, with friendly faces and a kind of hospitality that exudes midwestern warmth and genuine charm. It's the kind of place I'm proud to call home.

FORT WAYNE

THE HISTORIC CITY OF FORT Wayne shines from its perch at the convergence of three rivers— the St. Mary's, the St. Joseph, and the Maumee. Known as the Summit City, Fort Wayne was founded in 1794.

Two statues of prominent frontiersmen pay tribute to Fort Wayne's past. The city took its name from the flamboyant General Anthony Wayne (top), whose treaties with the region's Native Americans helped foster peace along the rivers. Although he successfully fought numerous battles against the Europeans, Chief Little Turtle (opposite) ultimately urged his Miami tribe to negotiate and end its fighting.

DUE IN LARGE PART TO THEIR prime geographical location, the lands around modern-day Fort Wayne have played a pivotal role in U.S. history. Such rich tradition comes alive again and again in local reenactments and parades.

T HAS BEEN A FEW HUNDRED years since General Anthony Wayne rode through town, but his legacy lingers in statues and buildings, such as downtown's Anthony Wayne Building (TOP LEFT). The heart of the city is also home to the Journal-Gazette Building (TOP RIGHT), constructed in 1871, and to Old City Hall Historical Museum (BOTTOM RIGHT). Built in 1893, the facility serves as headquarters for the Allen County-Fort Wayne Historical Society.

26

A MONG ITS MANY ATTRIBUTES, THE Foellinger-Freimann Botanical Conservatory always maintains proper pitch. Inside the glass structure, visitors can view three separate gardens, a gift shop, and hands-on educational displays. Keeping the wheels of business rolling in the area, the Greater Fort Wayne Chamber of Commerce operates out of offices on Ewing Street.

ALTHOUGH FORT WAYNE'S EARLY years were rife with territorial warfare, conflicts today are dealt with more civilly in the Allen County Courthouse (OPPOSITE).

Dedicated in 1902, the building is made of Indiana blue limestone and Vermont granite—punctuated by a copper-sheathed dome.

TWO WELL-KNOWN FACES ON the local political scene, former Mayor Paul Helmke (TOP) and Steve Shine (OPPOSITE) have a lot in common. Both men are active in the area's Republican Party—Shine is its chairman—and both are attorneys. Helmke, who served as the city's mayor from 1988 to 2000, is in private practice today, while Shine divides his time among politics, the law, and broadcasting.

BOTH THE FAMOUS AND THE common man find a place in Fort Wayne. One of the world's best-known Hoosiers is Abraham Lincoln, who lived in the state from 1816 to 1830. In his honor, the Lincoln Museum—under the guid-ance of President and CEO Joan Flinspach (OPPOSITE)—provides ac-cess to one of the largest collections of Lincoln materials, showcased in its 30,000-square-foot space on Berry Street.

ARCHITECTS AND ARTISTS HAVE left their marks on the development of Fort Wayne. A partner in the firm Martin Riley Mock Architects/Consultants, Victor Martin (RIGHT) has been instrumental in a new vision for the Baker Street train station, a historic arts and crafts building built in 1914 and currently under renovation. Works by painter Eldon Horner (LEFT) and sculptor Victor Garcia (OPPOSITE RIGHT) frequently appear around the city.

IT'S A DUESEY! TRANSPORTATION history is highlighted in several locations around the city. In nearby Auburn, the Auburn Cord Duesenberg Museum (BOTTOM) traces the development of the region's automobile industry during the 20th century. Teeming with memorabilia, the Greater Fort Wayne Aviation Museum (TOP) occupies a 6,000-square-foot site at the airport. Steam locomotive number 765 (OPPOSITE) was part of a fleet of 80 trains that offered fast freight service along the Nickel Plate Road line from Bellevue, Ohio, to Chicago. Under the auspices of the Fort Wayne Railroad Historical Society, the locomotive has traveled some 53,000 miles and pulled cars carrying more than 300,000 passengers on planned excursions throughout the eastern United States.

N EW STRUCTURES DOT THE FORT Wayne skyline, but the city's classic architecture still holds forth. The Cathedral of the Immaculate Conception (RIGHT) was dedicated in 1860 and underwent extensive interior renovation and restoration in 1998. The congregation of the First Presbyterian Church (LEFT) moved into its facility on Wayne Street in the 1950s. And the 22-story Lincoln Tower (OPPOSITE LEFT) was the city's first skyscraper, joined today by the modern, 26-story One Summit Square (OPPOSITE RIGHT).

THE JEWISH AND CATHOLIC FAITHS are among the many beliefs comprising Fort Wayne's religious community. The Most Reverend John D'Arcy (BOTTOM) is Bishop of the Fort Wayne-South Bend Diocese, while Rabbi Eddie Fox (OPPOSITE) guides the Congregation B'nai Jacob.

WHETHER VIEWED FROM ON HIGH or at street level, Fort Wayne bustles with the activity befitting Indiana's second-largest city.

Aʀт ɪᴍɪᴛᴀᴛᴇs ʟɪꜰᴇ ɪɴ ᴛʜᴇ ᴡᴏʀᴋs of Fort Wayne artist Eldon Horner, whose painting *Nightshift* (ABOVE) reflects an after-hours moment in the lobby of the Lincoln Life building. Reality, too, can offer its own quiet time (OPPOSITE).

EDICATED IN 1902, THE BEAUX arts Allen County Courthouse should be completely restored in time for its 100th anniversary. Work on the rotunda (OPPOSITE BOTTOM) was one of the first steps in the $11 million process, which began in 1995. Outside improvements included the leveling of several structures in front of the building to make way for a small park, known as Courthouse Green.

ORT WAYNE'S MANY ARCHITEC-
turally significant buildings
are rich in detail. Among them
is the 33-room Bass Mansion

(ABOVE). Completed in 1903, the
Romanesque masterpiece today
houses the University of Saint
Francis library.

Restrooms
← ← ←

CREATING THE AREA'S CLASSICAL dance lovers to three performances annually, the Fort Wayne Ballet is under the artistic direction of Karen Gibbons-Brown (ON RIGHT).

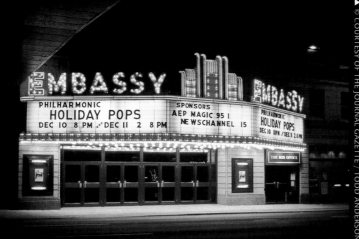

T HE LIGHTS GLEAM BRIGHTLY at Fort Wayne's renovated Embassy Theatre (THIS PAGE), but especially so during the holiday season. Aglow year-round, local philanthropist and female impersonator Charles "Tula" Miller (OPPOSITE) has established a reputation as a tireless fund-raiser for AIDS education and prevention.

BORN IN LENINGRAD TO A MUSICAL family, Fort Wayne Philharmonic Music Director Edvard Tchivzhel (ABOVE) defected to the United States while on tour in 1991. He joined the local organization in 1993, although he continues to serve as artistic director and advisor to the Auckland Philharmonia in New Zealand.

WHAT BETTER PLACE TO STAND face-to-face than under the heart-shaped arches of the bridal glen in Foster Park? Featuring nearly 255 acres of lush foliage, the park encircles an 18-hole public golf course.

THE FINEST IN FASHION AND A horse-drawn carriage help contribute to living happily ever after for local couples starting down the road to the future.

Growing up in Fort Wayne puts grins on the faces of many kids. Working to keep the smiles alive, the Fort Wayne Women's Bureau—led by President and CEO Dr. Betty Tonsing (opposite center)—supports a series of programs designed to help women with issues such as aging, employment, and family care.

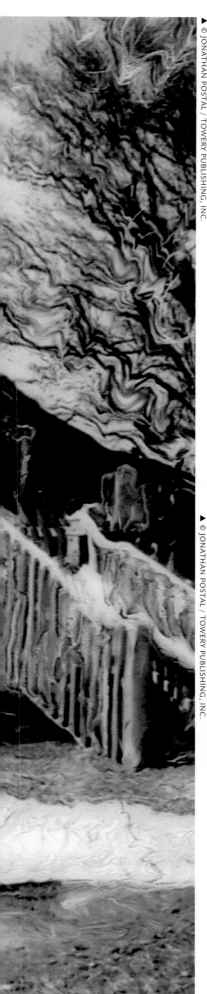

YOU DON'T HAVE TO BE AN EINSTEIN to enjoy Fort Wayne's Science Central. The hands-on interactive attraction—appropriately housed in the city's old electricity plant— relies on exhibits and displays to bring science, math, and technology within reach.

WITH 11 PUBLIC HIGH SCHOOLS and a host of private institutions, most of the teenage flipping done in Fort Wayne involves the pages of textbooks. The proof is in the test scores: Allen County's four public school districts consistently rank above national and state averages on standardized exams.

STRIVING FOR SUCCESS HAS become the hallmark of sports life in Fort Wayne. Under the guidance of Indiana University-Purdue University, Fort Wayne men's volleyball Coach Arnie Ball (RIGHT), the Mastodons have appeared in four NCAA Final Four tournaments since 1991.

© CHERYL A. FRTFIT

© LOUIS F. ROMAIN, MD

© JUDI PARKS

© JUDI PARKS

T RAINING TOPS THE BILL FOR FORT Wayne's workforce, whether on the street or on the stage. Sergeant Gary Stevens (LEFT) teaches police officers solid motorcycle skills, while Captain Dottie L. Davis (RIGHT) targets officers' shooting abilities. Directing altogether different casts are Al Franklin (OPPOSITE LEFT), executive director of the Fort Wayne Civic Theatre, and Larry L. Life (OPPOSITE RIGHT), chair and artistic director for the Department of Theatre at Indiana University-Purdue University, Fort Wayne.

KEEPING FORT WAYNE SAFE for its youth requires a wide range of action and intervention. Heartfelt memorials and supportive friends, family members, and law enforcement officers help get the anti-violence message across.

During the 1990s, Fort Wayne saw a dramatic downturn in violence and illegal drug activity. This reduction in crime was due in part to progressive law enforcement programs such as the Drug House Ordinance and in part to the cooperation between concerned citizens, public officials, and police officers.

INNER-CITY CHURCHES AND shelters—like Wings of Hope, a Christian halfway house for women—promote safety and community not only through their services and compassion, but sometimes even through the murals that decorate neighborhood buildings.

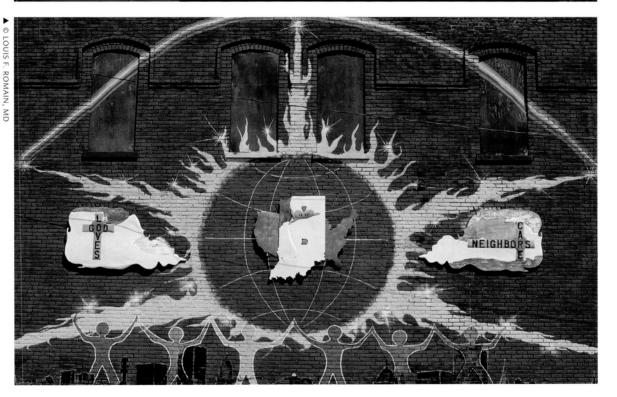

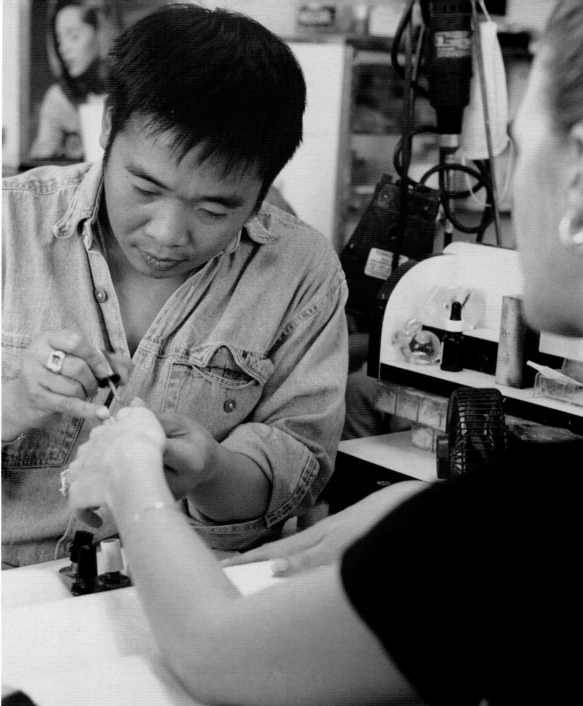

FROM THE ROOTS OF ITS EARLY Native American and European influences, Fort Wayne has emerged as a city that welcomes all and celebrates diversity.

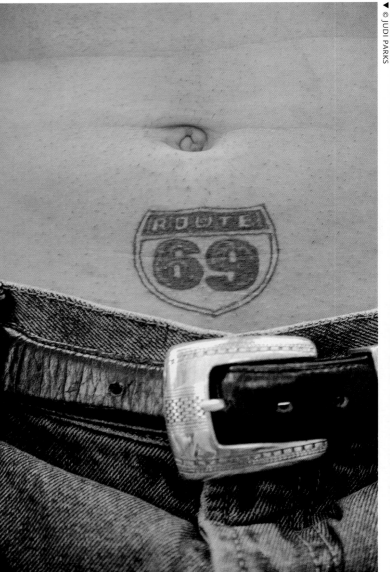

C OUNTER- AND SUBCULTURES thrive locally, with easy access to all the necessary bohemian accoutrements. At Studio 13, tattoo artist Nick Manco (TOP LEFT) leaves his mark on locals, while designs from the Modern Primitive are seen on various body parts all over the city. In addition, Rochelle (OPPOSITE) at Calhoun Street Antiques supplies patrons with a whimsical array of collectibles and vintage clothing.

THERE'S NOTHING RUSTY ABOUT Indiana's love for its nickname, the Hoosier State. In fact, the name appears prominently in a variety of locations, including an anti-smoking campaign funded by the nation's settlement with the tobacco industry.

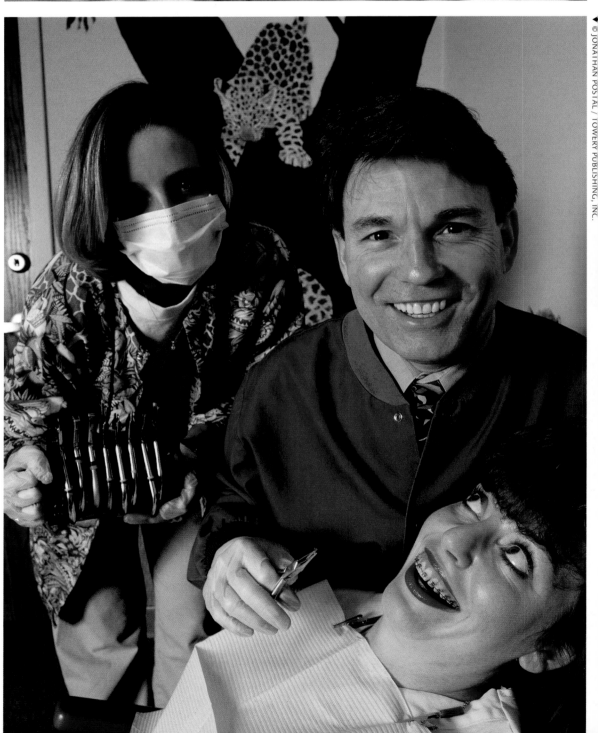

G ROWTH AND DEVELOPMENT ARE vital parts of the Fort Wayne landscape, but word of mouth has it that some locals are building other sorts of bridges. At the Matthew 25 Health & Dental Clinic (OPPOSITE TOP), doctors, nurses, and other staff members volunteer to provide free dental treatment to the city's poor and elderly. Local orthodontist Dr. Baron Whateley (OPPOSITE BOTTOM) and his staff focus on improving the area's smiles.

FORT WAYNE'S SKELETON DEPICTS a region on the move. From its earliest days as a prime portage location—it was commonly referred to as the "carrying place"—the city has grown to encompass nearly 75 square miles.

TALK ABOUT YOUR SMALL BUSINESS havens. Fort Wayne supports such establishments as the Tiny Tim Diner and Tiny Tune-Ups, but champions larger operations as well—many of them run by true men of steel.

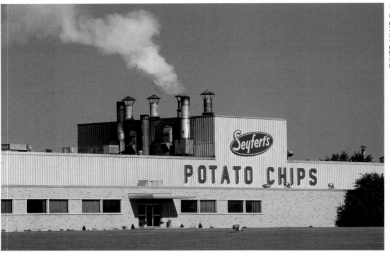

H ER APPEARANCE ON *THE TONIGHT SHOW* with Johnny Carson—named by *TV Guide* as the funniest moment in television history—made Myrtle Young (BOTTOM LEFT) a celebrity in her home city of Fort Wayne and beyond. A former inspector for the now-closed Seyfert's Potato Chips plant, Young has a world-renowned collection of potato chips shaped in the likenesses of the famous. A familiar local face in her own right, Little Miss Sunbeam (OPPOSITE) appears as the symbol for Sunbeam bread, which manufactures a number of its products at its Fort Wayne facility.

FORT WAYNE ENJOYS AN ENVI-
able reputation as the City of
Restaurants, and it lives up to that
designation with exquisite taste.
Run by Nike Spillson (ABOVE),
daughter of founder John Spillson,
the award-winning Café Johnell
serves up some of Indiana's finest
continental cuisine, with attentive
service and unsurpassed sophistication. For food that is less expensive
but no less tempting, the Mill Bread
Company (OPPOSITE) creates a
variety of fresh breads and pastries
each day, and has been ranked
among the nation's best bakeries
by *Modern Baking* magazine.

Klemm's
Kafe

BEST
BREAKFAST
IN TOWN!

CONEY ISLAND
SINCE 1914

OUR BUNS ARE STEAMED

THANK YOU
for Not Smoking

NO
SMOKING

s a local historic landmark.
he city's small cozy diners inspire
ot only those with voracious ap-
etites, but artists as well. Local
ainter Eldon Horner has made
ower's Diner the subject of one
f several of his Fort Wayne-
hemed pieces (ABOVE).

LOOKING TO BEAT THE HEAT, Fort Wayne screams for ice cream, especially the kind served by Zesto. But during the coldest months of the year, even Zesto can't compete with several feet of snow: The popular spot always closes during the winter.

$1.04 / 1.3

F ORT WAYNE'S NIGHTLIFE OFTEN consists of some combination of cocktails or cold beer and lots of good music. Strumming up the latter are local rockabilly combo the Blue Moon Boys (BOTTOM) and rock chanteuse Sunny Taylor (OPPOSITE BOTTOM), both of whom have garnered national acclaim.

ORT WAYNE'S MUSICAL ROOTS RUN
from blues to country to swing.
During the 1950s, Joe Taylor and
the Red Birds (OPPOSITE BOTTOM)—
featuring Joe Taylor and Patty
Corbett (OPPOSITE, TOP RIGHT)—
performed country swing in venues
throughout the region. Today's
listeners can get a dose of swing—
without the country—at the popular
Club Soda (OPPOSITE, TOP LEFT).

THE WISDOM THAT COMES FROM age plays an important role in Fort Wayne, where the curious can learn more about their ancestry at the renowned Genealogy Department of the Allen County Public Library (TOP RIGHT).

© BUD LEE

© JONATHAN POSTAL / TOWERY PUBLISHING, INC.

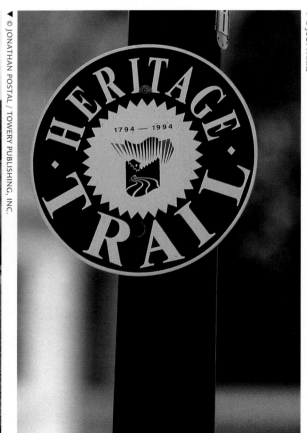

© JUDI PARKS

N RECOGNITION OF FORT WAYNE'S prominent role in the development of the United States, the African-American Museum (TOP) and the city's Heritage Trail—a self-guided tour of historical sites—provide a glimpse into the past.

EVEN THOUGH PHILO T. FARNS-worth was born in Utah and lived only a short time in Fort Wayne, residents consider the inventor an adopted son. His influence flickers in the thousands of television sets throughout Allen County, as well as in the Philo T. Farnsworth TV Museum (BOTTOM AND OPPOSITE BOTTOM). Located in Karen's Antique Mall, this tribute to early electronics joins such technological giants as General Electric Company (OPPOSITE TOP), which maintains a plant locally.

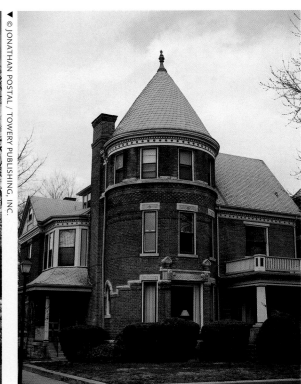

THE STAR OF NUMEROUS SILENT films and talkies alike, Carole Lombard—born in Fort Wayne in 1908—typified the glamour and charm of Hollywood in its glory days. Her birthplace, now known as the Carole Lombard House Bed & Breakfast, has been renovated to reflect the styles of the 1930s, and the inn's four guest rooms—including the Clark Gable Room (BOTTOM), named after her husband—honor a few of her Hollywood contemporaries. The house's sense of modest grandeur and luxury is echoed in stately residential architecture throughout the city.

ORT WAYNE WAS NAMED AN
All-America city in 1998, and
with its down-home charm shining
through, it's easy to see why. Allen
County's population—including an
undetermined number of folks with
green thumbs—topped the 315,000
mark in 2000.

THE FOELLINGER-FREIMANN Botanical Conservatory houses within its glass structures a menagerie of exotic plants and flowers. Opened in 1983, the facility has permanent displays of tropical rain forest flora and American Sonoran cacti. Each year, the conservatory hosts a number of seasonal displays, including the ever popular Fairy Gardens and a traditional Christmas show.

ESPITE THE PRESENCE OF GE-
netically enhanced crops and
state-of-the-art combines, many
fields are still harvested by hand
and horse-drawn equipment on
Amish farms around the region.

TRADITION THRIVES IN THE historic small towns and pristine farmlands around Fort Wayne. In Grabill, just a short drive from the city, H. Souder & Sons General Store (OPPOSITE) sells penny candy, homemade jams and preserves, fresh breads, and hand-sewn fabrics to visitors looking for an old-fashioned experience. Even further from the trappings of the big city, Indiana's natural attractions include lush forests, peaceful streams, and abundant wildlife (PAGES 118 AND 119).

ORT WAYNE'S OUTDOORS PRESENTS
a perfect environment for hunting and fishing, pastimes enjoyed
by residents of all ages.

W HAT BEGAN AS A HOBBY FOR BRAD and Karen Bonar (OPPOSITE) has become a real zoo. Married in 1982, the couple bought 13 acres of land and gradually added animals—both the everyday and the exotic kinds— to their farm. Today, the Black Pine Animal Park in Albion houses an ark's worth of rare, endangered, and retired animals. Attracting thousands of visitors each year, the park offers the rare opportunity to observe these animals in an open setting.

F ORT WAYNE CHILDREN'S ZOO teaches kids about animals and their environments through an array of detailed exhibits, as well as through the very popular Endangered Species Carousel. Run by Zoo Director Jim Anderson (OPPOSITE), the facility was named by *Child* and *Travel America* magazines as one of the best children's zoos in the nation.

WHETHER YOU'RE LOOKING FOR a quiet place to reflect, or an opportunity to immerse yourself in fun and games, Fort Wayne's 87 public parks offer pastoral retreats from the city's hectic pace.

ACH SEPTEMBER, FORT WAYNE celebrates the legacy of John Chapman—better known as Johnny Appleseed—with a popular festival that features vendors and performers in 1800s dress. At the core of all this activity is the festival namesake's grave site (OPPOSITE) in Archer Park, near the St. Joseph River.

WHILE ARTIST ELDON HORNER may have envisioned Fort Wayne as a paradise (OPPOSITE)— complete with serpents to tempt mankind—the real Eden might be the city's Foellinger-Freimann Botanical Conservatory, home of Woody the Talking Tree (TOP).

AKE NO MISTAKE: VIOLATORS will be prosecuted in Fort Wayne. Patrolling the city's 800-plus miles of roads and streets, some 340 police officers—and a few well placed signs—monitor parking regulations. Enforcement of a higher order is left to the individual.

STABLISHED IN 1839—ONE YEAR before Fort Wayne achieved official status as a city—the Fort Wayne Fire Department strives to prevent the loss of life and property. Its firefighters faced one of their greatest challenges in 1993, when historic St. Mary's Catholic Church (BOTTOM) was struck by lightning and caught fire. The resulting blaze toppled the tower and destroyed the building, but the church has since been rebuilt.

THE CATHEDRAL OF THE IMMACU-
late Conception (ABOVE) has
been guiding the spiritual lives of
many of the city's residents since
1859. But no amount of prayer
could keep long-time business

presence Lincoln National Insurance Company in town. Once one
of the area's largest employers, the
company moved its headquarters
to Philadelphia in 1999.

HOUSE PROTECTED BY ANGELS

KNOWN AS THE CITY OF CHURCHES, Fort Wayne represents a variety of beliefs and religions, all marked by strength and steadfastness. During every season, prayers of protection resound in houses of worship around the city.

S UN FILTERS THROUGH THE intricate panels of stained glass in Fort Wayne's Cathedral of the Immaculate Conception (ABOVE). The city's churches form the backbone of business for William L. Lupkin Designs, a stained-glass window studio run by Bill Lupkin (OPPOSITE, ON LEFT). He and his brother Steve (ON RIGHT) create and restore the colorful windows for residential and commercial clients around the country.

Text visible within the image: CHURCH of OUR LADY of PER- PE-TUAL HELP McCALL 1916-1964

REACHING OUT TO THOSE IN need, St. Mary's Soup Kitchen (TOP) provides nourishment for both the soul and the stomach. The kitchen survives and thrives, thanks to local and church volunteers— including St. Mary's pastor, Father Thomas O'Conner (BOTTOM)—who lend their time and energy to help fight the effects of home-lessness in Fort Wayne.

A MEMBER OF FORT WAYNE'S leadership community, Reverend J.W. Bledsoe serves as pastor for St. John Missionary Baptist Church, one of the city's most prominent African-American churches.

SACRED HEART

MEDICAL PROFESSIONALS GIVE their time and talent to heal others, but Joyce Roush (ABOVE), a local nurse and coordinator for the Indiana Organ Procurement Organization, has given much more. In 1999, she donated one of her kidneys to a Maryland boy she had never met. Joseph Ladowski, M.D. (OPPOSITE) takes his mission to heart as well: He's a cardiovascular and thoracic surgeon at Fort Wayne-based Indiana/Ohio Heart.

I T'S ALL IN THE LINE OF DUTY for firefighters such as Steve Koenes and for Parkview Hospital's Samaritan helicopter crew. With one chopper in Fort Wayne and a second stationed in Rochester, the organization's emergency vehicles soar above city streets on missions that can make the difference between life and death.

FORT WAYNIANS HAVE LONG had a fascination with flight, and the city celebrates annually with hot-air balloon festivals. Dirigible fever struck the area early: The German-owned Graf Zeppelin (OPPOSITE TOP) flew over Allen County on its 1929 world tour.

W HATEVER THE OCCASION, FORT Wayne knows how to turn on the fireworks and otherwise light up the night sky. From holiday decorations to Three Rivers Festival explosions, the city celebrates in style.

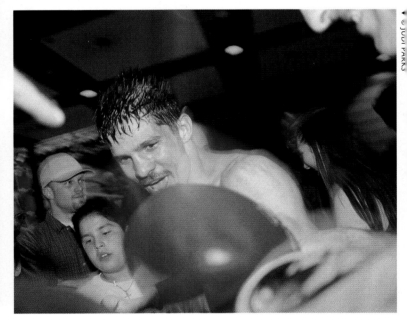

ORT WAYNIANS GET A KICK OUT OF just about any sport, be it baseball or kick boxing. The city hosts a full roster of minor-league teams, including the Class-A Wizards (OPPOSITE, TOP LEFT AND RIGHT), a farm team for the San Diego Padres; the United Hockey League Komets (LEFT); and the ever popular Fort Wayne Fury of the Continental Basketball Association. After leading the Fury to two consecutive winning seasons—a first in the franchise's history—head coach Keith Smart (OPPOSITE, BOTTOM LEFT) left Fort Wayne to serve as assistant coach for the Cleveland Cavaliers.

FORT WAYNE'S AVID GOLFERS aren't just Sunday drivers. Whether inside or out, they are dedicated to the pastime, as evidenced by the activity on the city's more than 20 public courses, as well as on private links like the Sycamore Hills Golf Club (TOP AND OPPOSITE TOP). Even Indiana Governor Frank O'Bannon (BOTTOM) gets in on the action at the annual Mad Anthony's Celebrity Golf Tournament.

DOWNTOWN HAS BECOME A nucleus of activity in Fort Wayne, thanks in part to public spaces like Freimann Square (THIS PAGE), which some locals say affords the best view of the skyline.

Spanning 22 acres along the St. Mary's River, nearby Headwaters Park (OPPOSITE) hosts a number of events each year, including the Three Rivers Festival.

FORT WAYNE

LET'S GO SWIMMIN'

© JONATHAN POSTAL / TOMLEY PUBLISHING, INC.

REVEALING QUITE A DIFFERENT view of Fort Wayne, riverboat tours along the St. Mary's, St. Joseph, and Maumee recall the city's storied past, as well as its undying spirit.

FORT WAYNE
CITY *of* SPIRIT

A LOOK AT THE CORPORATIONS, BUSINESSES, PROFESSIONAL GROUPS, AND COMMUNITY SERVICE ORGANIZATIONS THAT HAVE MADE THIS BOOK POSSIBLE. THEIR STORIES—OFFERING AN INFORMAL CHRONICLE OF THE LOCAL BUSINESS COMMUNITY— ARE ARRANGED ACCORDING TO THE DATE THEY WERE ESTABLISHED IN THE FORT WAYNE AREA.

ACORDIA/O'ROURKE ◆ ALMET, INC. ◆ BARRETT & MCNAGNY, LLP ◆ BEERS MALLERS BACKS & SALIN, LLP ◆ BUDGET RENT A CAR OF FORT WAYNE ◆ CANTERBURY GREEN ◆ CENTRAL SOYA COMPANY, INC. ◆ CONNOR CORPORATION ◆ COVINGTON COMMONS SENIOR COMMUNITY ◆ DESIGN COLLABORATIVE ◆ DON R. FRUCHEY, INC. ◆ ELLISON BAKERY INC. ◆ FEDERATED MEDIA ◆ FORT WAYNE/ALLEN COUNTY CONVENTION AND VISITORS BUREAU ◆ FORT WAYNE RADIOLOGY/FORT WAYNE RADIOLOGY MRI CENTER/OPEN VIEW MRI ◆ FORT WAYNE WIRE DIE, INC. ◆ GENERAL CREDIT UNION ◆ GREATER FORT WAYNE CHAMBER OF COMMERCE ◆ HOLIDAY INN NORTHWEST/HOLIDOME ◆ ICON INTERNATIONAL ◆ INDIANA UNIVERSITY-PURDUE UNIVERSITY FORT WAYNE ◆ INTERNATIONAL BUSINESS COLLEGE ◆ INTERNATIONAL PARK ◆ IVY TECH STATE COLLEGE ◆ MEDICAL IMAGING ◆ THE MEDICAL PROTECTIVE COMPANY ◆ MIDWEST AMERICA FEDERAL CREDIT UNION ◆ MIDWEST TOOL & DIE CORPORATION ◆ PARKVIEW HOSPITAL ◆ PEG PEREGO, U.S.A., INC. ◆ PHD, INC. ◆ PHELPS DODGE MAGNET WIRE COMPANY ◆ REDiMED ◆ STEEL DYNAMICS, INC. ◆ SWEETWATER ◆ TOKHEIM CORPORATION ◆ WAYNE COMBUSTION SYSTEMS ◆ WOODBURN DIAMOND DIE, INC. ◆ WPTA-TV 21ALIVE ◆

FORT WAYNE
CITY *of* SPIRIT

GREATER FORT WAYNE CHAMBER OF COMMERCE

S THE CITY'S ADVOCATE FOR BUSINESS GROWTH, THE Greater Fort Wayne Chamber of Commerce has been a solid partner with area businesses since 1875. The regional center, with a staff of 25, services Allen County, where Fort Wayne is located, as well as the eight surrounding counties: Adams, DeKalb, Huntington, LaGrange, Noble, Steuben, Wells, and Whitley.

The chamber's principal purpose involves promoting the Fort Wayne area to new business and helping existing business to prosper. "We're the primary advocate for the growth and expansion of the private sector of Northeast Indiana," says Phil Laux, president and CEO. "We're recognized within the community and the surrounding areas as an impact player."

MORE THAN A CENTURY OF SERVICE

The chamber originated in 1875 as the Fort Wayne Commerce Club, and its original mission was to aid business growth in the city. In 1918, the club reorganized as the Fort Wayne Chamber of Commerce.

Just six years later, the chamber decided to build its own facility and, today, that original building is still in use. According to Laux,

Fort Wayne is one of the few communities in the country with a chamber that doesn't lease space in an office building. "And that's the way it should be," he says. "This is the community's building." Currently, the chamber makes its facilities available to civic groups, member companies, and other community organizations for meetings, wedding receptions, and other events.

Throughout Fort Wayne's vibrant past, the chamber has played an essential role in developing business relationships and enhancing the business climate of the community. Laux points to two periods in which the chamber played a critical role in the growth and vitality of the community, raising large funds to attract new business to the area.

In 1983, after International Harvester closed the doors on its Fort Wayne operations, leaving the economy and thousands of employees stranded, the chamber went to work on behalf of the city. Its efforts netted dozens of smaller

FOR ALMOST A CENTURY, THE GREATER FORT WAYNE CHAMBER OF COMMERCE HAS SERVED THE REGION FROM ITS HISTORIC HEADQUARTERS ON WAYNE AND EWING STREETS IN DOWNTOWN FORT WAYNE.

to midsize companies that relocated to the area, as well as General Motors Truck and Bus Group, now one of the city's top five employers. A second strong campaign brought additional smaller and midsize companies to town in the late 1980s.

COMPETITIVE FORT WAYNE

In the race for new business, Fort Wayne competes against other cities in Indiana, Ohio, and Michigan. Although Indiana leads an aggressive quest for new business, the state is set to become even more competitive with its incentives in the future.

When attracting new companies to the Fort Wayne area, the chamber looks at the types of jobs and wages each company offers. Currently, it is focusing on bringing more technology-based companies to the area. But that doesn't necessarily mean recruiting software companies. Instead, the chamber will consider more companies that concentrate on technology-based solutions that include advanced manufacturing processes.

For numerous reasons, Fort Wayne is an ideal location for many different types of businesses, making the city an easy product to sell. First, the cost of living is low. Unemployment insurance and workers' compensation are also extremely reasonable. And

Fort Wayne is strategically located in the geographical center of the country. In fact, the city lies within 300 miles of 25 to 30 percent of the population of the United States, which makes it perfectly suited for companies that rely on transportation to do business.

Although it has a primarily manufacturing-based economy, Fort Wayne has emerged over the past few years as a medical hub. "If you were to combine all of the hospitals, physician groups, and insurance groups," says Laux, "the medical industry would represent the most significant segment in Fort Wayne." Fort Wayne is also a retail and entertainment hub for Northeast Indiana.

Appropriately, the city's economic makeup reflects diverse industries. According to a recent report compiled by the chamber,

Fort Wayne's top employers include, from largest to smallest, Fort Wayne Community Schools (FWCS), General Motors Truck and Bus Group, Lincoln Financial Group, Dana Corporation, Parkview Health System, GTE, ITT Aerospace Communications Division, the City of Fort Wayne, Raytheon Systems Co., and Allen County Government.

Numerous awards have been bestowed upon the city to commemorate its high quality of living. For five consecutive years, Fort Wayne was listed in *Industry Week*'s top 10 communities. In 1997, ReliaStar, a Minneapolis-based financial company, ranked Fort Wayne number three in the country for offering residents the greatest opportunity for financial security. In 1998, the city was given the All-America City award for a

CLOCKWISE FROM TOP LEFT: LOCAL OFFICIALS RECENTLY BROKE GROUND FOR THE DALMAN ROAD EXPANSION, WHICH WILL PROVIDE DIRECT ACCESS BETWEEN FORT WAYNE INTERNATIONAL AIRPORT AND I-69.

"FORT WAYNE IS A PROGRESSIVE, REGIONAL CENTER," SAYS PHIL LAUX, PRESIDENT AND CEO. "THIS IS A COMMUNITY THAT ISN'T CONTENT TO LIVE IN THE PAST, FOR ITS EYE IS ON THE FUTURE."

IN RECENT YEARS, THE CHAMBER HAS PARTNERED WITH THE FORT WAYNE-ALLEN COUNTY AIRPORT AUTHORITY TO MARKET FORT WAYNE INTERNATIONAL AIRPORT. THE NEW FORT WAYNE INTERNATIONAL AIR TRADE CENTER OPENED IN 1999 AND IS HOME TO KITTY HAWK CARGO.

FORT WAYNE WAS NAMED 1999
COMMUNITY OF THE YEAR BY
THE INDIANA STATE CHAMBER
(TOP).

ONE OF THE GREATER FORT
WAYNE CHAMBER OF COMMERCE'S
TOP PRIORITIES IS COMMUNITY
INVOLVEMENT. IN 1999, CHAMBER
STAFF RESTORED LANDSCAPING AT
COMMUNITY HARVEST FOOD BANK
AS PART OF THE UNITED WAY
DAY OF CARING (BOTTOM).

second time; it had previously received this award in 1983. In addition, it received the Indiana State Chamber's Community of the Year award in 1999.

SIX DIVISIONS

The chamber devotes its resources mainly to six initiatives for improving conditions for existing and incoming businesses: economic development, workforce development, government and community affairs, small business, membership, and communications. The goal of economic development, for example, involves attracting additional investment to the community by bringing new companies to the area or helping businesses expand.

In addition, the workforce development division heads up resources such as the Career Connection program, which educates area students about job opportunities and provides actual work-based learning experience. Fort Wayne Community Schools, along with hundreds of volunteers from the higher education community and private sector, helped create and implement the program when community members became alarmed at the low rate of high school students pursuing vocational school or higher education and at the even lower rate of students who completed their advanced schooling. The program has been such a success at FWCS that the chamber is currently working to duplicate it in the other school systems in Allen County.

The government and community affairs division employs a full-time lobbyist who works with the local legislative delegation to ensure that area businesses are being represented in the government and that bills are passed to help, rather than hinder, them. Laux describes the chamber's role in working with Fort Wayne's elected community as an initiator: "We bring the local units of government to

the table and put the right packages together," he says.

Efforts of the small business division are concentrated on developing and implementing programs and services for the small business membership. Programs include Business Expo, Northeast Indiana's largest business exposition. The annual show, which meets at the Allen County War Memorial Coliseum, provides an opportunity for companies to advertise their goods and services, in addition to offering valuable seminars and featured speaker presentations. The division also offers monthly and quarterly programs designed for small-business and minority members.

The membership branch works to retain and expand the number of members in the chamber. Currently, the chamber has approximately 2,000 members, which represents 35 to 40 percent of the businesses in the area. Although the chamber would like that number to increase, according to Laux, in comparison to membership numbers of other chambers around the country, Fort Wayne's membership base is strong.

Finally, the communications staff works to inform the Greater Fort Wayne area about chamber events through a monthly periodical called *Emphasis* and a weekly fax update. Ground breakings for new facilities and ribbon-cutting ceremonies for expansions are also coordinated through this division.

There are also several organizations that either report to the chamber or were established through the chamber and have now formed their own organizations. For example, the chamber is the host organization for Indiana Northeast Development Corporation, a regional economic development group, as well for the Small Business Development Center, which is funded by the Small Business Administration (SBA). The World Trade Association and the Fort Wayne Sports Corporation, on the other hand, started as committees of the chamber and are now their own entities.

MARKS OF SUCCESS

The chamber has continuously campaigned for the prosperity of

Fort Wayne and the surrounding areas. Most recently, it has been involved with the growth of the Fort Wayne International Airport. In fact, certain members of the chamber's staff carry only one responsibility: to market the Fort Wayne International Airport and the Air Trade Center.

The Air Trade Center is a 450-acre industrial park adjacent to the Fort Wayne International Airport with taxiway access to a 12,000-foot runway, one of the longest in the Midwest, all built exclusively for aviation-related business. The center is an established foreign trade zone, so companies can operate duty free. One of its first tenants was Kitty Hawk Cargo, the world's largest nonintegrated air freight carrier and the leading U.S. provider of air freight charter logistics services. Kitty Hawk, which occupies a $35 million cargo sort facility, moves 1 million tons of freight a night.

Air passenger service has been another focus of the chamber. With the help of the chamber staff, working in conjunction with the airport's marketing staff, passenger services in Fort Wayne have been greatly expanded. Growing numbers of major airlines now offer regional jet service at the airport with more flights leaving and arriving in Fort Wayne daily. Expansion continues as the chamber and the airport's marketing staff bring more passengers and airlines to the airport.

Another mark of the chamber's success is the Dalman Road expansion project, which resulted from the united efforts of the chamber, city and county

officials, and state legislators. The project is a 3.5-mile extension of a road that will connect major interchanges in southwest Allen County. Thanks to this project, economic development will be boosted in southwest Allen County, and accessibility to the Fort Wayne International Airport will be greatly enhanced.

One of the chamber's most recent undertakings involves the Northeast Indiana Innovation Center, which will be located near the campus of Indiana University-Purdue University at Fort Wayne. The center is being designed as a technology incubator. Says Laux, "We're providing an environment to foster the entrepreneurial spirit of Fort Wayne."

The chamber recognizes that one of the most recent challenges in continuing Fort Wayne's economic growth has been the lack of industrial parks for light to medium-sized users. Although large chunks of land are available for large-scale businesses, all of

the local industrial parks for users who require smaller space are filled. Businesses that need a 30,000- to 50,000-square-foot parcel have had to look in other cities. Laux says in the near future, land will be opened in the area for these types of businesses.

AN EYE ON THE FUTURE
As for the future, Laux believes Fort Wayne will eventually consider restructuring its government. The current organization, which consists of city and county officials, was born in the 1800s and hasn't been modified to suit the times. Also, Fort Wayne will continue to diversify its economic base. In spite of the recent rash of mergers and acquisitions that have affected companies around the country, Fort Wayne has continued to grow.

According to Laux, that shows promise for the future. "Fort Wayne is a progressive, regional center," he says. "This is a community that isn't content to live in the past, for its eye is on the future."

PARTICIPATION IN THE ANNUAL BUSINESS EXPO PROVIDES EXPOSURE FOR LOCAL COMPANIES (TOP LEFT AND RIGHT).

HOSTED BY THE CHAMBER'S WORKFORCE DEVELOPMENT DIVISION, JOB EXPO PROVIDES AN OPPORTUNITY FOR LOCAL STUDENTS TO MEET WITH POTENTIAL EMPLOYERS (BOTTOM).

Barrett & McNagny, LLP

ORT WAYNE'S HISTORY IS TIED TO BARRETT & McNagny, LLP, one of the oldest and largest firms in Northeast Indiana. For more than a century, the firm has worked to promote its clients, many of them Fort Wayne business leaders and community organizations, to the pinnacle of success.

In 1876, James Madison Barrett joined Charles H. Aldrich to form Aldrich & Barrett. In 1925, Phil McNagny joined the firm, which then became known as Aldrich, Barrett & McNagny. In 1986, the firm officially became Barrett & McNagny.

In 1987, the firm moved to its current location on Berry Street in a building that is as much a part of Fort Wayne history as Barrett & McNagny. Once known as the Elektron Building, it was built in 1895, and is listed today in the National Historic Registry. From 1898 to 1902, it served as the Allen County Courthouse. In 1904, the building housed the Allen County Public Library while a permanent library was under construction. Lincoln National Life Insurance Company adopted the Elektron

Building as its headquarters from 1912 to 1923.

One of Barrett & McNagny's greatest assets is a history in Fort Wayne that dates back more than 100 years. Doing business so long in the city makes the firm's attorneys better able to understand the local marketplace and assist their clients.

UNDERSTANDING CLIENTS' NEEDS

Today, Barrett & McNagny continues to play an important role in Fort Wayne's development.

Since its founding, the firm has helped establish and sustain many of the area's leading businesses and public institutions. Barrett & McNagny works primarily with clients from the business community, including banks, utilities, insurance companies, health care providers, manufacturers, and media companies, together with many small and medium-sized companies. These clients are located mainly in Fort Wayne and northern Indiana, although several have operations worldwide.

Barrett & McNagny offers its clients a full range of legal services. Specialty areas include business and real estate; employment and labor relations; employee benefits; environmental; estate planning and administration; finance, securities, and taxation; health care; litigation and dispute resolution; media and communications; and bankruptcy and creditors' rights.

The firm assists companies as they form new businesses; buy and sell real estate; finance development; solve employment problems; comply with environmental laws

THE CENTER OF LEGAL ACTIVITY
IN THE AREA, THE ALLEN COUNTY
COURTHOUSE (TOP) IS UNDERGO-
ING AN $8 MILLION RENOVATION
TO RESTORE THE BUILDING TO ITS
ORIGINAL GRANDEUR. SCHEDULED
TO BE COMPLETED IN 2002—THE
100TH ANNIVERSARY OF THE
COURTHOUSE'S DEDICATION—THE
RESTORATION WILL REMOVE
DECADES OF PAINT AND SOOT,
AND WILL REPAIR MAJOR DAMAGE
TO THE GRAND ROTUNDA, THE
DOME (BOTTOM LEFT), AND THE
COURTROOMS.

and other state and federal regulations; execute retirement plans
and health plans; protect copy-
rights and trademarks; collect debts;
and resolve business disputes and
conflicts through negotiation, arbi-
tration, trials, and appeals. Its
attorneys also provide personal
legal services, including adoptions,
wills, trusts, and estate planning
and administration.

Barrett & McNagny remains
committed to its clients by offering specialized legal services. The
firm recruits attorneys with the
expectation that they will develop
a specialty and become expert in
a particular area of law. By developing this expertise, the firm can
better serve the diverse needs of
its clients. Clients discover that
Barrett & McNagny provides them
efficient, affordable, high-quality
legal representation, continuing
the tradition of excellence the
firm has developed.

COMMITTED TO COMMUNITY

Just as Barrett & McNagny has
contributed to Fort Wayne's

growth, so too has Fort Wayne
helped mold the firm into what
it is today. The firm feels that
Fort Wayne is a community
with good people and good val-
ues, which translates into good
business practices. The firm also
feels that it is a privilege to do
business with the people who
live and work in this community.

The attorneys and other personnel at Barrett & McNagny
take active roles in the community, many of them volunteering
as leaders in various organizations. The firm also supports
the community through donations of pro bono legal time,

and each year it selects different
ways to support various community organizations.

Barrett & McNagny's lead-
ership extends into the legal community as well. Throughout the
firm's history, it has had various
attorneys serve as the president
of the Indiana State Bar Association, as well as other offices at
the national, state, and local levels.

The challenge for the future
is to maintain the high standards and quality that have been a
Barrett & McNagny tradition.
Through that commitment, the
legal needs of the firm's clients
will be well served.

ONE OF BARRETT & MCNAGNY'S
GREATEST ASSETS IS A HISTORY IN
FORT WAYNE THAT DATES BACK
MORE THAN 100 YEARS. DOING
BUSINESS SO LONG IN THE CITY
MAKES THE FIRM'S ATTORNEYS
BETTER ABLE TO UNDERSTAND THE
LOCAL MARKETPLACE AND ASSIST
THEIR CLIENTS (BOTTOM RIGHT).

PARKVIEW HOSPITAL

PARKVIEW HOSPITAL'S NAME IS SYNONYMOUS WITH caring, compassion, and community. For more than 120 years, this not-for-profit organization has reached out to improve the health of its neighbors in Fort Wayne and surrounding counties. ◆ It originated in 1878 as the Fort Wayne City Hospital.

After two name changes, the facility was rebuilt and rechristened Parkview Hospital in 1953. Today, the 520-bed, regional medical center belongs to the Parkview Health System, a regional network of health care providers working together to improve medical care, promote community health, and reduce the cost of services.

REGIONAL CENTERS AND AIR RESCUE TEAM

Parkview's strengths include a Regional Trauma and Emergency Center, which treats about 70,000 people each year. In fact, it is one of the busiest trauma centers in the Midwest. Working closely with the Parkview Samaritan helicopter service, the center receives many transfer patients because of its high level of expertise.

Since its debut in 1989, the air rescue team has combined the staff and technology of a trauma center with the speed and mobility of a helicopter service. There are two helicopters—one based in Fort Wayne and the other in Rochester, Indiana—that cover northern Indiana, western Ohio, and southern Michigan.

Parkview has also earned an excellent reputation for its Regional Heart Center and Regional Cancer Center. Both facilities bring new research treatment to Northeast Indiana, so patients do not have to travel far to access the latest treatments and medications.

Other important areas of Parkview's services include the Regional Orthopedic Center; the Diabetes Treatment Center of Parkview; the Regional Neurological and Rehabilitation Center; the New Life Center, featuring 46 private rooms for new mothers; Parkview Behavioral Health; Parkview Hospital's Regional Children's Center, now one of the largest in Northeast Indiana; and Parkview Stucky Research Center.

CHARACTERIZED BY COMPASSION

Although Parkview is a high-tech hospital committed to bringing leading-edge treatments to its patients, it is also a hospital with a sense of compassion for the local community. As such, Parkview partners with several community organizations to help people at risk and people who are disadvantaged. Its staff believes a hospital that is more involved in and more accessible to the community is a more effective one. As a result, Parkview has always been a strong supporter of Matthew 25 and other health clinics in the area.

Parkview has also joined the Fort Wayne Community Schools (FWCS) to provide school nurses and medical social work staff for nine area schools. In addition, it has sponsored funding and supplies for the YWCA domestic violence shelter and the Baby's Closet, a community program that encourages low-income, expectant mothers and new parents to practice good prenatal and postpartum care.

Parkview creates partnerships not only with community organizations, but also with other health care providers. Most recently, for example, Parkview partnered with Cameron Hospital in Angola to develop a cancer treatment center in that part of Indiana.

All of Parkview's efforts reflect the hospital's ongoing mission to make health care available to as many people in the region as possible. Undoubtedly, this tradition will continue for years to come.

THE 520-BED PARKVIEW HOSPITAL HAS REACHED OUT TO IMPROVE THE HEALTH OF ITS NEIGHBORS IN FORT WAYNE AND SURROUNDING COUNTIES.

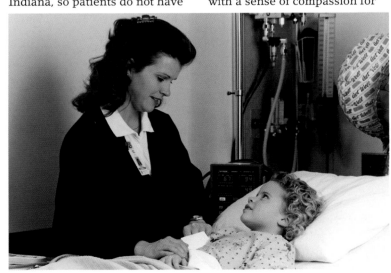

PARKVIEW'S MISSION IS TO "PROVIDE QUALITY HEALTH SERVICES TO ALL WHO ENTRUST THEIR CARE TO US, AND TO IMPROVE THE HEALTH OF OUR COMMUNITIES."

TUDENTS WHO ATTEND INTERNATIONAL BUSINESS College know their futures are in good hands. The school not only graduates students with bachelor's degrees in 30 months, but also boasts a high graduation rate for its students. ◆ The second oldest business college in Indiana, International Business

College was founded in 1889 by Thomas Staples, who came to Fort Wayne via Ontario, Canada, where he had established the first of six international colleges. In 1969, Bradford Schools, Inc. acquired the local operation. Today, International Business College is affiliated with nine other Bradford colleges in Charlotte, North Carolina; Chicago, Illinois; Columbus, Ohio; Houston, Texas; Indianapolis, Indiana; Minneapolis/ St. Paul, Minnesota; New York, New York; Pittsburgh, Pennsylvania; and St. Louis, Missouri.

Between its day and evening classes, International Business College educates approximately 800 students every year, 80 percent of whom attend classes directly after high school, and most of whom live within a 120-mile radius of the Fort Wayne campus. Although housing has been available for women since 1970, the school's residence facility became open to men as well in September 1999.

EDUCATION FOR THE WORKFORCE

A nationally accredited institution, International Business College confers diplomas, associate degrees, and bachelor's degrees in 11 disciplines: accounting, administrative support, business administration, computer applications and programming, finance, graphic design, industrial management, legal studies, medical assisting, retailing, and travel and hospitality. All of these programs are geared toward ensuring good entry-level positions for students once they graduate.

At International Business College, students can take courses in their area of concentration immediately, rather than wading through a series of non-major classes. In fact, many students take only a few general courses throughout their studies. From the start, students are trained for

the workforce. "If students complete only 10 months of college and receive a diploma, they'll have had courses in their major and will be more marketable to prospective employers," says Jim Zillman, president of International Business College in Fort Wayne and its affiliate in Indianapolis.

Classes at the college strive to duplicate the environment students will encounter in the workplace. A dress code, for example, prohibits sneakers, jeans, and shorts. Instead, students dress in casual business attire. Attendance is enforced with a policy that prohibits students from missing more than 10 percent of their classes.

A DEDICATED PLACEMENT OFFICE

One of International Business College's greatest strengths is its post-graduation job placement program. In fact, successful job placement is often the primary reason students choose to attend the college. Experienced placement coordinators share the responsibility of finding career positions for every student who graduates. The office also makes its services available to alumni.

In addition, International Business College has established a strong rapport with hundreds of businesses in Fort Wayne and surrounding cities. Because local employers are so pleased with students from the college, many

companies want to be first to interview graduates.

Building on more than a century of success in Fort Wayne, the school's proven strength in placement is right in line with the vision of Thomas Staples, who, in establishing International Business College, sought to empower students with the necessary tools to shape their own futures.

THE MEDICAL PROTECTIVE COMPANY

A PART OF THE GENERAL ELECTRIC (GE) FAMILY OF companies, The Medical Protective Company is a Fort Wayne-based provider of professional liability insurance for physicians, dentists, and health care organizations. When the company was formed at the end of the 19th century, it revolutionized the medical industry by inventing professional liability insurance for physicians. At that time, medical malpractice was rare. Yet, when physicians were sued, they found legal counsel inadequate to protect their interests.

In 1899, a team of physicians partnered with Byron Somers, an attorney, to create The Medical Protective Company. The company earned its reputation as a successful defender of physicians' rights against allegations of malpractice. Defense, however, was only part of the strategy. In 1909, Medical Protective became the first company to pay damages, thus marking the start of medical malpractice insurance.

A privately held company for most of its history, Medical Protective continued to grow and prosper quietly. By the late 1960s, it was one of the leading companies of its kind in the country, providing coverage to almost 100,000 physicians, surgeons, and dentists.

In the 1970s, Medical Protective faced a formidable challenge in the shifting world of malpractice. No longer was it unusual for patients to sue doctors, and soon, the number of suits and the size

of awards increased. Many other companies that provided professional liability coverage collapsed under pressure. Medical Protective, however, survived, thanks to its financial strength, commitment to health care, and experience. In fact, Medical Protective was one of the few companies that continued to write new business during that time.

In October 1998, Medical Protective became part of GE. As a GE business, it is part of the world's most admired company, according to a 1999 *Fortune* magazine survey. According to Tim Beck, president and CEO of Medical Protective, the acquisition by GE is yet another mark of the company's success. "When the Employers Reinsurance Corporation (ERC) Group decided to grow its health care business, it only looked at one company," he says, "and that was us."

LEADER IN MEDICAL MALPRACTICE INSURANCE

Today, Medical Protective is the oldest medical malpractice insurance company in the country. It offers coverage to physicians, dentists, and, as of the mid-1990s, hospitals in 30 states, al-

though it holds licenses in every state except New York. With approximately 33,000 physicians as clients, Medical Protective is the country's largest malpractice insurance company in terms of the number of physicians served. It is also the second-largest provider of malpractice insurance to dentists—currently insuring some 23,000.

In addition, Medical Protective provides risk management services that include information resources, such as a quarterly newsletter, *Protector*, which was created in the 1920s, and a regularly updated Web site; risk management program development; self-assessment tools; safety, security, and regulatory compliance services; an event-tracking system; on-the-spot consultation; and educational services.

Since its beginning, Medical Protective has worked to be the best in medical malpractice, and there's every indication the company is meeting that goal. For the past several years, Medical Protective has been ranked by Ward's Financial Group as one of the top 50 property and casualty companies in the country. The firm has also consistently earned excellent

THE MEDICAL PROTECTIVE COMPANY IS A FORT WAYNE-BASED PROVIDER OF PROFESSIONAL LIABILITY INSURANCE FOR PHYSICIANS, DENTISTS, AND HEALTH CARE ORGANIZATIONS.

ratings from A.M. Best and Standard & Poor's. In fact, Standard & Poor's has referred to Medical Protective as the Cadillac of the medical malpractice business.

In 1995, Flaspohler Rose Marketing Research Inc. conducted a national medical malpractice survey and ranked Medical Protective as the best professional liability underwriter in the United States. Its criteria included financial strength, integrity of contract and policy language, service, and defense expertise.

FINANCIAL STABILITY AND EMPLOYEE KNOWLEDGE

Medical Protective's strengths today are the same attributes that have carried the company to success since its founding. Beck cites financial stability—now an even greater asset since GE Capital acquired Medical Protective—as the firm's number one strength. Because the medical industry is so volatile, physicians, dentists, and hospitals want to make sure they're with a financially sound company. Medical Protective has prided itself for years on its financial stability, achieving its goal of being one of the most secure insurance providers in the country.

A talented pool of employees also defines Medical Protective as an industry leader. In Fort Wayne, the company employs approximately 220 people. In its 28 other offices around the country, it employs 150. Medical Protective has a very low turnover rate, and a majority of its employees have been with the firm 10 to 20 years. "Our employees' experience in dealing with malpractice and providing the best defense for doctors is a crucial component in our success," Beck says.

COMMUNITY INVOLVEMENT

As part of GE, Medical Protective is set to begin a new era of community involvement. In the past, the Byron Somers Foundation donated large sums of money anonymously to local charities and foundations. Currently, Medical Protective is a United Way company and a sponsor of Focus on Health, and plans to become more involved in the communities it serves.

MEDICAL PROTECTIVE'S FUTURE ALSO INCLUDES PLANS FOR SIGNIFICANT GROWTH, NOT ONLY IN FORT WAYNE, BUT ALSO AROUND THE COUNTRY (TOP).

WITH APPROXIMATELY 33,000 PHYSICIANS AS CLIENTS, MEDICAL PROTECTIVE IS THE COUNTRY'S LARGEST MALPRACTICE INSURANCE COMPANY IN TERMS OF THE NUMBER OF PHYSICIANS SERVED. IT IS ALSO THE SECOND-LARGEST PROVIDER OF MALPRACTICE INSURANCE TO DENTISTS—CURRENTLY INSURING SOME 23,000 (BOTTOM).

Medical Protective's future also includes plans for significant growth. In the coming years, the company plans to provide insurance coverage in all 50 states and to double its premium volume. As it moves forward with these initiatives, The Medical Protective Company expects to grow in Fort Wayne, as well as in various locations across the country.

BEERS MALLERS BACKS & SALIN, LLP

BEERS MALLERS BACKS & SALIN, LLP IS A FULL-SERVICE LAW FIRM THAT ENGAGES IN THE PRIVATE CIVIL PRACTICE OF LAW AND HANDLES ALL LEGAL MATTERS THAT AFFECT ITS CLIENTS' BUSINESS, PERSONAL, AND PROFESSIONAL LIVES (LEFT).

ACCORDING TO JOHN W BOWERS, THE FIRM'S MARKETING PARTNER, BEERS MALLERS BACKS & SALIN HAS PLAYED AN IMPORTANT ROLE IN SHAPING THE FUTURE OF ITS CLIENTS: "WE'VE BEEN INTEGRAL TO THE SUCCESS OF MANY OF OUR CLIENTS, AND THAT'S THE MOST REWARDING PART" (RIGHT).

ONE MEASURE OF BEERS MALLERS BACKS & SALIN, LLP'S SUCCESS IS ITS LONGEVITY. IN 2001, THE LAW FIRM WILL CELEBRATE ITS 100TH ANNIVERSARY, MAKING IT, AS the adage suggests, older but wiser. Beers Mallers Backs & Salin is a full-service law firm that engages in the private civil practice of law. Its clients range from individuals to Fortune 500 companies, and it handles all legal matters that affect its clients' business, personal, and professional lives. Although most of its clients reside in Indiana, Ohio, and Michigan, several are located in other states around the country, as well as in Europe and Canada.

Since 1901, the law firm has been an integral part of the Fort Wayne community. In fact, Beers Mallers Backs & Salin has represented Allen County, Indiana, in legal matters since the early 1960s. As Fort Wayne has grown throughout the years, so too has Beers Mallers Backs & Salin.

A CENTURY OF SUCCESS

The firm was originally founded as Kennerk & Somers, although the name changed several times over the next few decades. In 1984, the merger of two smaller firms—Dumas Backs Salin & Vegeler (originally Kennerk & Somers) and Adair Perry Beers Mallers & Larmore, each with a variety of specialties—led to the creation of a full-service law firm. In 1989, the firm officially became known as Beers Mallers Backs & Salin. The firm opened a second office in LaGrange, Indiana, in 1994.

Today, the Beers Mallers Backs & Salin team consists of 23 attorneys and 23 staff members, with 41 of these team members working in the Fort Wayne office. Peter Mallers is the managing partner; Vincent Backs is the senior partner; William Fishering, who has been Allen County attorney since the mid-1980s, is a partner; and Kurt Bachman is a resident partner in LaGrange.

The firm's attorneys currently practice in several specialty areas. They include the following: business and corporate law, corporate collections, creditors' rights and bankruptcy, elder law, environmental law, estate planning and administration, intellectual property, labor and employment relations, litigation, municipal law, and real estate.

As is common with many law firms, if a special legal problem arises where its attorneys don't have the necessary expertise, Beers Mallers Backs & Salin will contract with another firm regionally or nationally that possesses the special legal expertise to meet its clients' needs. Likewise, Beers Mallers Backs & Salin has often been hired as special counsel by other law firms.

NURTURING THE ENTREPRENEURIAL SPIRIT

Since 1989, the firm has more than doubled in size. Today's legal matters are becoming more complicated, which requires greater devotion to specialty areas of

practice. According to John W Bowers, the firm's marketing partner, Beers Mallers Backs & Salin has played an important role in shaping the future of its clients. "We've been integral to the success of many of our clients, and that's the most rewarding part," he says, adding that the firm's attorneys are sensitive to the needs of their own clients because many of them have hired attorneys for their own business and personal matters.

Several years ago, one of the firm's clients started a business in his garage with his sons. Today, that client has more than 200 employees and exceeded $100 million in sales in 1999. "Fort Wayne has been home to a number of entrepreneurs. We've helped many of them incorporate, grow, and seek investment moneys," Bowers says.

That commitment to its clients has driven the firm's success for

decades. "We work to deliver the highest-quality legal work at extremely competitive prices," Bowers says. "We demand the best of ourselves, and our clients demand it of us."

DRIVEN BY EXCELLENCE

Beers Mallers Backs & Salin is also devoted to professionalism in the law. In the back of its main brochure, Solomon is quoted as saying, "A good name is to be valued more than good wealth." As Bowers explains, "We value our reputation and our character, and because of that, we strive to afford our clients, staff, and attorneys the opportunity for excellence."

Opportunities for excellence abound at the law firm. Staff members and attorneys are encouraged to grow professionally while maintaining a balance with their family life. "We're proud that we've established and maintained a

family-oriented environment. We're committed to our families, churches, synagogues, and other organizations, and the firm has allowed us to maintain that level of participation in other areas of life besides law," says Bowers.

In addition, the firm has a long-standing tradition in the political arena. Several of its attorneys have been active in politics, serving as precinct committee chairs and GOP county chairmen for more than three decades. The firm is also the legal home of a former U.S. congressman and a former U.S. ambassador.

Bowers foresees that Beers Mallers Backs & Salin will continue to grow well into the future. In fact, the firm recently occupied additional space in its downtown National City Center offices, and hired new full-time attorneys. As it expands, the firm will work to maintain a balance between legal success for its clients and personal growth and development, within and outside the law firm. Beers Mallers Backs & Salin will undoubtedly remain, as it has for the past century, one of Fort Wayne's most loyal and successful business members.

CLOCKWISE FROM TOP:
SINCE 1901, BEERS MALLERS BACKS & SALIN HAS BEEN AN INTEGRAL PART OF THE FORT WAYNE COMMUNITY. IN FACT, IT HAS REPRESENTED ALLEN COUNTY, INDIANA, IN LEGAL MATTERS SINCE THE EARLY 1960S.

THE FIRM'S EXECUTIVE COMMITTEE INCLUDES (FROM LEFT) PETE MALLERS, VINCE BACKS, RICK BEERS, AND BILL FISHERING.

BEERS MALLERS BACKS & SALIN WILL UNDOUBTEDLY REMAIN, AS IT HAS FOR THE PAST CENTURY, ONE OF FORT WAYNE'S MOST LOYAL AND SUCCESSFUL BUSINESS MEMBERS.

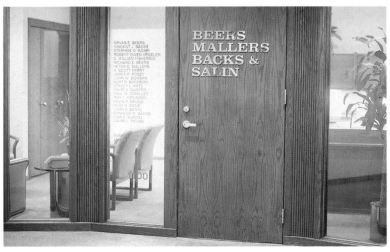

TOKHEIM CORPORATION

ORE THAN A CENTURY AGO, TOKHEIM CORPORATION introduced the world's first gas pump. Today, the company enjoys success as the world's largest designer and manufacturer of fully electronic, computer-linked petroleum dispensing devices and systems, including pay-at-the-pump terminals and retail automation systems.

Headquartered in Fort Wayne, the publicly held corporation, whose common stock is listed on the New York Stock Exchange, boasts $750 million in annual sales and employs 4,800 people worldwide, with 722 employees working in Fort Wayne. Its global manufacturing facilities are located in Fremont, Indiana; Washington, Indiana; Lancaster, Pennsylvania; Denver, Colorado; Chesapeake, Virginia; France; Scotland; the Netherlands; South Africa; and Germany. All of Tokheim's facilities are ISO 9000 certified.

Douglas K. Pinner, chairman, president, and CEO, heads an executive team that includes Jacques St-Denis, executive vice president of operations; Robert L. Macdonald, executive vice president of finance and CFO; and Norman Roelke, vice president, secretary, and general counsel.

A HISTORY OF INNOVATION
In 1898, John J. Tokheim invented a pump to dispense kerosene and gasoline. By 1901—thanks to the popularity of what became the Tokheim Dome Oil Pump— the Tokheim Manufacturing Company was established in Iowa.

Two businessmen from Fort Wayne, Ralph Diserens and M. B. Muxen, purchased Tokheim Manufacturing in 1918 and moved it to Fort Wayne, renaming the company Tokheim Oil Tank and Pump Company. Fort Wayne was a natural home for Tokheim, since two of the original leading pump companies were also located in the city. In fact, during the early 1900s, more pumps were produced in Fort Wayne than anywhere else in the world.

The company officially became known as Tokheim Corporation in 1953, and since then has introduced to the industry numerous

creative innovations that have secured its position of technological leadership. Tokheim developed the first underground gas storage with the company's original dome pump, the first mechanical computing system on a gas pump in 1934, and the first electronic computing pumps in 1974. In the late 1970s, Tokheim was the first dispenser company to introduce liquid crystal display (LCD) as a user interface. Tokheim introduced multi-product dispensers for customer convenience and efficient gas island flow in the early 1980s. Almost a decade later, Tokheim introduced credit card readers in dispensers, facilitating customer payment on the gas island. The company brought to the market a blender dispenser in the early 1990s. Blenders allow retailers to minimize underground tanks and reduce the number of meters in the dispenser. In the mid-1990s, Tokheim released a series of innovative products ranging from wireless communications and radio frequency identification to Windows NT-based point of sale systems.

The company is in the process of releasing a new touchscreen-based user interface for dispensers.

IN 1998 AND 1999, THE PETRO-
LEUM EQUIPMENT INSTITUTE
(PEI), AN INTERNATIONAL TRADE
ASSOCIATION FOR DISTRIBUTORS,
MANUFACTURERS, AND INSTALLERS
OF EQUIPMENT USED IN PETROLEUM
MARKETING, HONORED TOKHEIM
WITH ITS MANUFACTURER OF THE
YEAR AWARD (TOP).

IN 1998, TOKHEIM CORPORATION
WAS NAMED THE OFFICIAL FUEL
DISPENSER FOR THE INDIANAPOLIS
MOTOR SPEEDWAY, HOME OF THE
INDY 500. TOKHEIM PUMPS HAVE
BEEN FUELING INDY RACE CARS
SINCE 1936 (BOTTOM).

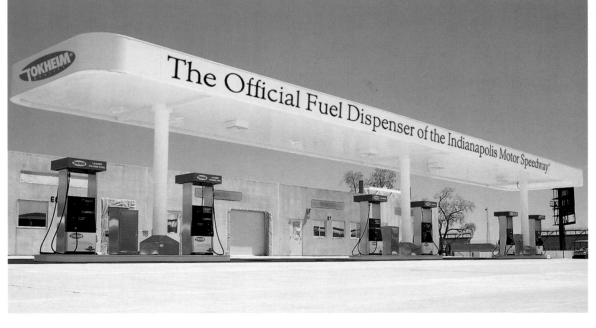

This flexible unit will support merchandising on the island and will serve as a user-friendly, comprehensive diagnostic tool for reduced cost of ownership. Tokheim continues to use its industry standard positive displacement meter; however, at the turn of the century, a new metering technology—the axial flow meter—will be utilized.

GROWTH THROUGH ACQUISITIONS

Due to its $434 million commitment to acquisitions, Tokheim has experienced tremendous growth and success. In 1986, Tokheim purchased Gasboy International, a manufacturer of commercial dispensers and farm pumps. Sofitam International, a France-based manufacturer of petroleum dispensers, became Tokheim's next acquisition in 1996. Although Tokheim had already established a presence in North and South America, Asia Pacific, and eastern and central Europe, the merger with Sofitam allowed Tokheim to increase its material presence in southern Europe and Africa.

In 1998, Tokheim acquired Management Solutions Inc. of Denver, a point of sale company that provides retail automation solutions. Several months later, Tokheim purchased Retail Petroleum Systems, a $350 million division of Schlumberger Ltd., doubling Tokheim's size and significantly enhancing the product development, global manufacturing, distribution, service, and employee strengths of the combined company.

These acquisitions have made the difference in keeping Tokheim ahead of its competition. "To stay at the top, we have to be global in nature," says Pinner. "Through acquisitions and subsequent resource integration, we are now able to offer global solutions to global clients at the highest standard of excellence."

According to Pinner, approximately 30 percent of Tokheim's business is domestic; the remaining 70 percent is overseas. Its clients are divided into several categories. Tokheim supplies major oil companies such as Amoco and BP Oil, as well as regional oil companies, like Speedway and Super America, that sell inside the United States. Tokheim also supplies jobbers—gas stations that carry a national brand but are owned by individuals—and convenience stores.

A COMMITMENT TO QUALITY AND DISTRIBUTION

The quality of its products and its people separates Tokheim from its competitors. "It is because of the demanding standards our employees set for themselves that we can offer the highest-quality product in the industry," Pinner says. "The integrity and loyalty of our employees, coupled with our technological expertise, have enabled us to put programs in place that best anticipate and meet the needs of our clients." Tokheim continues to implement practices to increase product quality and enhance the health and safety of its employees. According to Pinner, "Each year, we strive to raise the bar on how we measure excellence."

Over the years, Tokheim has established the largest global distributor network in the industry, with 414 distributors and more than 319 authorized service organizations. The majority of sales are channeled through district offices and a large network of independent petroleum equipment firms. In addition, Tokheim has sales representatives located around the world.

In recognition of the company's support of its distributor network, Tokheim was awarded the Manufacturer of the Year Award in 1998 by the Petroleum Equipment Institute (PEI), an international trade association for distributors, manufacturers, and installers of equipment used in petroleum marketing. For three consecutive years, PEI has recognized Tokheim for its excellence. In 1996 and 1997, Tokheim received PEI's Circle of Excellence Top Five Finalists Award. In addition, in 1998, the company was named the official fuel dispenser for the Indianapolis Motor Speedway, home of the Indy 500. Tokheim pumps have been fueling Indy race cars since 1936.

As Tokheim gears up to enter its second century of operation, it will continue to grow. Tokheim already commands $750 million of the industry's $2.2 billion in volume, and its strategic emphasis in the future will be on greater efficiency and extending the company's leadership position by every measure. "In four brief but intense years, we have moved the company from $160 million in sales to industry leadership with more than $750 million in volume," Pinner says. "We recognized the mandate for a global presence, and our organization rose to the challenge of achieving that goal. There is much more to be done, and the opportunities are only limited by the limits of our vision. Our global presence notwithstanding, Fort Wayne, Indiana, will always remain a major hub for us." That's good news for the community, for each acquisition means new jobs and new opportunities for Fort Wayne.

TODAY, TOKHEIM ENJOYS SUCCESS AS THE WORLD'S LARGEST DESIGNER AND MANUFACTURER OF FULLY ELECTRONIC, COMPUTER-LINKED PETROLEUM DISPENSING DEVICES AND SYSTEMS, INCLUDING PAY-AT-THE-PUMP TERMINALS AND RETAIL AUTOMATION SYSTEMS.

FOR THE PAST 75 YEARS, ACORDIA/O'ROURKE HAS BEEN one of Fort Wayne's most loyal business citizens. It not only attracts employees to the area, but also provides insurance and risk management services that help hundreds of businesses in Fort Wayne and surrounding areas achieve success. ◆ William

S. O'Rourke Jr. founded the business, O'Rourke & Company, in 1923, and ever since, the insurance broker has grown through acquisitions and mergers. In 1968, when it merged with J.E. Maroney, Inc., the firm was renamed O'Rourke & Maroney, Inc. Three years later, the name again changed to O'Rourke, Andrews & Maroney, Inc., due to the merger with Andrews & McFadden, Inc.

Most important, in 1994, the firm became part of the Indianapolis-based Acordia, Inc., the world's largest privately held insurance broker. With an employee base of 3,000-plus people and more than 80 locations across the United States, Acordia recorded $308.9 million in revenues in 1998. Frank C. Witthun is president and CEO of Acordia, Inc.

O'Rourke, Andrews & Maroney joined the Acordia family to maintain the long-term viability of the

company. "We needed to position ourselves so that we had access to resources to respond to our clients' needs," says President and CEO William G. Niezer, who is also the founder's grandson. "We are now able to offer a broader array of products and services to our clients." Acordia/O'Rourke employs a staff of 80 in Fort Wayne.

PLAYING A PART IN CLIENTS' SUCCESS

As a full-service insurance broker, Acordia/O'Rourke provides property and casualty insurance, workers' compensation, employee benefits, and retirement benefits. The majority of its clients are midsize businesses located in the Fort Wayne and Allen County area, although Acordia/O'Rourke does work with clients around the country and overseas.

Those services continue to expand as the needs of the broker's clients grow. "The more we can do for the client, the more we can control the outcome of the process," Niezer says. Consequently, Acordia/O'Rourke has established an in-house claims administration department to assist its clients. In addition, for several decades, the company has maintained a loss-prevention and safety services department staffed by certified safety engineers. "When clients place their business with us," Niezer adds, "we can provide them with all the services to meet their needs."

Although its name has changed throughout the years, Acordia/O'Rourke's business philosophy has not. "It's our customers who account for our success," Niezer says. "With our services, we've helped companies grow and become successful, and that has

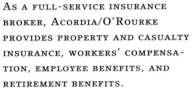

AS A FULL-SERVICE INSURANCE BROKER, ACORDIA/O'ROURKE PROVIDES PROPERTY AND CASUALTY INSURANCE, WORKERS' COMPENSATION, EMPLOYEE BENEFITS, AND RETIREMENT BENEFITS.

allowed us to grow and become successful."

Many clients have partnered with Acordia/O'Rourke for 50-plus years, and the longevity of its client base defines Acordia/O'Rourke's success. "During that time, account responsibilities have been handled by a variety of people, so the common link must be the attitude and approach we take to the business," Niezer says. "Clearly, those clients must be satisfied with our approach to have continued doing business with us for so long." In fact, those clients have often referred Acordia/O'Rourke to business colleagues and friends. Those referrals are also another way to measure success: As Niezer says, "Referrals are the firm's lifeblood."

FAMILY AND COMMUNITY INVOLVEMENT

In addition to its client base, family plays a large part in the company's history. Niezer is the third generation in his family to work in the agency, following his father, Bernard M. Niezer, who preceded him as president. Several other families also claim a long past with the company. Gerald C. Kramer Sr. worked with Niezer's grandfather and father, and today, Kramer's son, Jerry, works for the company. Such is also the case with Richard Ryan, who worked with Niezer's father; today, Ryan's son, John, works at Acordia/O'Rourke. These families, as well as Acordia/O'Rourke's other employees, have learned that the firm nurtures growth and excellence. "We've created a culture wherein our people view their employment as a career as opposed to a job," Niezer says. "I'm proud to be a part of an organization that has survived throughout the years and has made such a difference in the community."

Acordia/O'Rourke prides itself on its more than 75-year relationship with the community. "Because Fort Wayne has fueled our growth, we make every effort to support the community's events and organizations," Niezer says. Whether that means providing financial support or encouraging

employees to volunteer for various community activities, Acordia/O'Rourke considers itself an active, involved member of the community.

In the next several decades, Acordia/O'Rourke will build on its tradition of adapting to the needs of its clients. "The O'Rourke

organization has always been viewed as a leader in the industry, and I expect we will continue to set the standard," Niezer says. "I'd like to believe that we'll continue to be a recognized and respected insurance broker in the Fort Wayne community for a long time."

FAMILY PLAYS A LARGE PART IN ACORDIA/O'ROURKE'S HISTORY. PRESIDENT AND CEO WILLIAM NIEZER (STANDING) IS THE THIRD GENERATION IN HIS FAMILY TO WORK IN THE AGENCY, FOLLOWING HIS FATHER, BERNARD M. NIEZER (SEATED), WHO PRECEDED HIM AS PRESIDENT.

INTERNATIONAL PARK

INTERNATIONAL PARK IS A PHOENIX RISEN FROM THE ashes. The complex was built in 1923 to accommodate the needs of International Harvester, once Fort Wayne's largest employer with more than 10,000 employees. But on September 27, 1982, International Harvester announced that it was shut-

ting its doors in Fort Wayne, leaving thousands of stunned individuals without jobs and vacating one of the city's largest industrial spaces.

NEW OWNERS, NEW USES
In 1985, principals of Covington Capital and SL Equities acquired the property. They have established a niche in industrial real estate, particularly in renovating and redeveloping corporate America's dinosaurs, says Larry Pregon, vice president of Quadrelle Realty Services, which has managed International Park since 1985.

To turn the building into a multiuse, multitenant complex, the owners spent millions of dollars on renovations. Improvements included reroofing, adding loading docks, parceling the buildings into smaller spaces, installing individual heating units, providing separate utility meters, improving roadways within the complex, demolishing functionally obsolete buildings, and renovating the buildings' exteriors.

Currently, Wayne Coliseum Limited Partnership owns the property, and Fort Wayne-based property manager Jan Jackson oversees the complex. Jan's father, Doug Jackson, worked as the property manager for Inter-

national Park for more than 10 years. The complex utilizes the services of local professionals, contractors, and employees in its day-to-day operations.

BRINGING BUSINESS TO INTERNATIONAL PARK
Today, International Park boasts 1.5 million square feet of usable space. The complex occupies 130 acres, with about 20 to 30 acres available for further development.

The complex is suited for industrial and warehousing tenants, including retail, light manufacturing, and office clients. Presently, a diverse mix of

60 to 70 tenants occupies about 90 percent of the space, employing close to 1,500 people and breathing new life into a complex that has a rich history in Fort Wayne. International Park has developed a reputation as an excellent starting location for new businesses and a place to grow. Many of the park's larger tenants began as start-ups that have grown to become major employers in Fort Wayne.

Whereas warehousing tenants dominated the complex initially, taking advantage of the affordable space, International Park now has a wide variety of tenants ranging from color card manufacturers to T-shirt makers. The tenant mix has shifted in favor of manufacturing- and assembly-type tenancies, which typically employ more highly skilled labor than warehousers.

To attract prospective tenants to the complex—whether they are located in Indiana or out of state—Quadrelle works closely with the local brokerage community and government agencies, such as the Greater Fort Wayne Chamber of Commerce and Northeast Indiana Economic Development. Quadrelle also markets International Park in its available site listings on its Web page, www.quadrelle.com. Cur-

INTERNATIONAL PARK IN FORT WAYNE IS SUITED FOR INDUSTRIAL AND WAREHOUSING TENANTS, INCLUDING RETAIL, LIGHT MANUFACTURING, AND OFFICE CLIENTS.

INTERNATIONAL PARK IS WELL KNOWN FOR ITS DISTINCTIVE TOWER, WHICH IS A LANDMARK FOR MANY IN FORT WAYNE, AND FOR ITS REPUTATION AS A FACILITY WITH A CAN-DO ATTITUDE.

rently, the company manages more than 20 million square feet of industrial real estate nationwide.

Another important factor in leasing space is International Park's reputation and recognition in the community. The complex is well known for its distinctive tower, which is a landmark for many in Fort Wayne, and for its reputation as a facility with a can-do attitude. The owners are proud of their ability to swiftly consummate a transaction, and they are quick to recognize a tenant with potential, as well as willing to take risks on tenants who may not be welcome at other facilities.

THREE BIG ADVANTAGES

Locating to International Park presents several advantages to potential tenants. First, the facility has direct rail access, a unique amenity not always available to industrial complexes.

International Park's size is obviously another benefit, as this allows tenants to expand as needed. In fact, it is not unusual to find a tenant who started with 7,200 square feet upgrading to as much as 150,000 square feet. "We're proud of our ability to accommodate tenants' needs, from the smallest to the largest footage," Pregon says.

Affordability also drives businesses to International Park. "Our rates are very competitive," says Pregon, adding that the communal atmosphere of the complex often attracts businesses. It is com-

mon, for example, to find one tenant utilizing the products or services of another, as well as tenants assisting one another in their daily routines.

FORT WAYNE'S CONTRIBUTION

Fort Wayne has played its part in making International Park a success. "Any facility this size, no matter where it is, needs the support of the surrounding community and government," says Pregon. "Fort Wayne laid the groundwork to make this property a success." He cites a thriving economy, a strong labor force, and a track record of small businesses flourishing in this area as key components of International Park's success. "International Park is probably one of the most successful industrial redevelopments in the Midwest," Pregon says.

In addition, the cooperation of city, county, and state governments was a key factor in the facility's redevelopment. Indiana provides incentive packages for businesses to relocate to the area. And, recently, International Park was designated by the Fort Wayne City Council as an economic revitalization area, making companies in the complex eligible for a tax abatement on the purchase of new machinery.

As International Park continues to evolve, upgrades and renovations will be undertaken to ensure the complex meets the needs of its tenants. Specific goals for the future include making additional exterior improvements and constructing new buildings on the remaining undeveloped acres. As Pregon says, "We'll always be looking to improve International Park. To benefit it is to benefit Fort Wayne."

CLOCKWISE FROM TOP LEFT: INTERNATIONAL PARK NOW HAS A WIDE VARIETY OF TENANTS RANGING FROM COLOR CARD MANUFACTURERS TO T-SHIRT MAKERS. THE TENANT MIX HAS SHIFTED IN FAVOR OF MANUFACTURING- AND ASSEMBLY-TYPE TENANCIES, WHICH TYPICALLY EMPLOY MORE HIGHLY SKILLED LABOR THAN WAREHOUSERS.

TO TURN THE BUILDING INTO A MULTIUSE, MULTITENANT COMPLEX, QUADRELLE REALTY SERVICES OVERSAW THE EXPENDITURE OF MILLIONS OF DOLLARS ON RENOVATIONS, SUCH AS ADDING LOADING DOCKS.

INTERNATIONAL PARK HAS DEVELOPED A REPUTATION AS AN EXCELLENT STARTING LOCATION FOR NEW BUSINESSES AND A PLACE TO GROW. MANY OF THE PARK'S LARGER TENANTS BEGAN AS START-UPS THAT HAVE GROWN TO BECOME MAJOR EMPLOYERS IN FORT WAYNE.

UCCESSFUL RADIO STATIONS MIRROR THE TASTES, INTER-ests, and attitudes of their communities. That's why the six stations owned by Federated Media are all top rated in Fort Wayne. ◆ Federated Media opened in 1959 when its owner, the late John Flint Dille II, and his son John Flint Dille III purchased

two radio stations and one television station in Fort Wayne. After the Dilles sold the television station in 1971, they bought additional radio interests in Grand Rapids, Cincinnati, and Tulsa, as well as a newspaper in Elkhart, Indiana. With the success of Federated Media's two Fort Wayne radio stations, Dille III decided to concentrate exclusively on Indiana, so he sold all the out of state radio holdings.

In 1993, Federated Media purchased K105; in slightly more than a year's time, the country station soared to the number one ranking. The company subsequently purchased WOWO in 1994, WBYR in 1996, and WFWI in 1997. Today, those four stations, as well as two of the original stations, WMEE and WONO, make up Federated Media.

Each of the company's six stations emphasizes a different format: news talk, 24-hour sports talk, classic rock, adult contemporary, rock, and country. This strategy has many advantages,

according to Tony Richards, who serves as general manager of four of the six stations, along with Bob Schutt, general manager of WFWI and WBYR. For example, Federated Media can consolidate its resources, employ a strong sales force, and effectively meet the diverse needs of listeners and advertisers in Fort Wayne and surrounding areas. "We used to concentrate on how we could make each station the best and beat the competition," says Richards. "Now when we look at each station, we look at its effect on the entire market and determine if the audience is being served."

Federated Media also works to stay up-to-date with the latest technology. In 1998, the company invested more than $500,000 to computerize all its operations. Rather than facing broken CD players or editing on tape machines, Federated Media's 120 employees can now complete all their work by computer.

No matter how much Federated Media invests in technology, though, there's still one basic element that fuels its success: the on-air personalities at each station. "We have the best broadcasters in Fort Wayne," Richards says. And he should know: From 1982 to 1991, Richards and Charly

FEDERATED MEDIA'S SOUTH COMPLEX IS HOME TO FOUR OF THE COMPANY'S SIX POPULAR RADIO STATIONS: WOWO 1190 AM, WMEE 97.3, WQHK 105.1 FM (ALSO KNOWN AS K105), AND WONO 1380 AM.

TONY RICHARDS (LEFT) SERVES AS COO FOR FEDERATED MEDIA AND GENERAL MANAGER FOR FOUR OF THE COMPANY'S SIX STATIONS, WHILE BOB SCHUTT IS GENERAL MANAGER OF WBYR 98.9 FM AND WFWI 92.3 FM.

Butcher hosted the market's number one-rated morning show on WMEE, called *Those 2 Guys in the Morning*. In 1987, more than one-third of the people in Fort Wayne and the surrounding area listened to their show every day.

WOWO 1190 AM

For 75 years, people in Fort Wayne have depended on WOWO almost as much as they depend on their utility companies. WOWO first broadcast in 1925 and today is Indiana's only 50,000-watt AM radio station, which means that its signal can be broadcast hundreds of miles. In fact, in the evenings, WOWO's signal has been heard in countries as far away as Finland and France.

Throughout the years, several unique features have given the station its distinctive personality, adding to its rich history. When WOWO was located in downtown Fort Wayne, radio personalities looked out at the fire escape to report the weather. Today, that fire escape is world famous.

Back then, radio was in its prime, and it wasn't uncommon to find up-and-coming musical groups debuting on the air. *Hoosier Hop*, for example, was one of WOWO's first hit shows, playing the music of Judy and Jen, Don and Helen Bush, and the Blackhawk Valley Boys. Another popular WOWO show was *The Little Red Barn*, which ran from 1945 until 1997. The show featured musical entertainers like the Oregon Rangers, who later became known as Nancy Lee and the Hilltoppers.

In 1945, the station introduced the Penny Pitch, a community fund-raiser developed by broadcaster Sam DeVincent, and Jay Gould, WOWO's farm director at the time. Created to help a needy family, Penny Pitch has since grown into a miniature version of United Way, providing assistance to families throughout Allen County. Although Penny Pitch is held year-round, it receives the most attention during the Thanksgiving and Christmas seasons, when collection cans for change are displayed at area businesses. WOWO also runs

special promotions for Penny Pitch by hosting on-air auctions, placing collection barrels at Fort Wayne Komets hockey games, and pumping gas for change.

Annually, Penny Pitch raises anywhere from $20,000 to $100,000, which Federated Media's board of directors distributes to local charities. In 1997, for example, WOWO raised $30,000.

Because Allen County is the largest agricultural county in the state, WOWO earns half its revenue from farm-related business. The station reports commodities and marketing closings daily, and employs a full-time farm director, Kevin Morse. WOWO is also a member of the National Association of Farm Broadcasters.

In addition to the farm reports, WOWO features news talk radio, attracting a mostly male crowd aged 30 to 54. In a day's time, listeners can tune in to local shows

like *Macy in the Morning* with Dave Macy, *WOWO Sports Talk* with Art Saltsberg and Dean Pantazi, and the *Pat White Show*. WOWO also features national personalities Rush Limbaugh and Dr. Laura Schlessinger, and is the local radio affiliate for the Indianapolis Colts, the Fort Wayne Komets, University of Notre Dame football, and Indiana University basketball.

Twenty counties around Indiana and Ohio rely on WOWO for notification of school delays and closings, but that's just part of the station's commitment to its hometown. "WOWO is always there for Fort Wayne," Richards says. "We are truly Fort Wayne's station."

WONO 1380 AM

Known locally as The Game, WONO is devoted to 24-hour-a-day coverage of sports. WONO

TO EFFECTIVELY MEET THE DIVERSE NEEDS OF LISTENERS AND ADVERTISERS IN FORT WAYNE AND THE SURROUNDING AREA, FEDERATED MEDIA EMPLOYS A STRONG SALES FORCE THAT INCLUDES (FROM LEFT) TONY RICHARDS; LESLIE GOODWIN, K105 SALES MANAGER; LEANN BROWN, WMEE SALES MANAGER; AND MARK DEPREZ, DIRECTOR OF SALES FOR FEDERATED MEDIA SOUTH (TOP).

WOWO OFFERS A VARIETY OF NEWS TALK SHOWS, INCLUDING *Macy in the Morning* WITH DAVE MACY (CENTER). JOINING HIM IN THE STUDIO ARE JIM TIGHE THE WEATHER GUY (LEFT) AND MICHARL O'SHEA, NEWS DIRECTOR (RIGHT).

Federated Media believes its employees—including (clockwise from top) Pat Thomas, 92.3 The Fort's evening personality; Jim Fox, WBYR program director; WONO SportsRadio personality Gary the Guy from The Game; and Keith Harris, WFWI program director—are the key to the company's popularity and success.

switched its format in March of 1998 to focus on sports, complementing WOWO's existing coverage.

Currently, the station primarily attracts a male audience aged 25 to 54 and broadcasts Fort Wayne Fury basketball, Fort Wayne Wizards baseball, and Indiana University football, as well as high school football and basketball. The station also hosts sports call-in shows. For fans who want up-to-the-minute scores, The Game features sports flashes every 20 minutes throughout the day.

WFWI 92.3 FM
Under Federated Media's ownership since 1996, WFWI, also known as The Fort, has flourished by defining itself as a classic rock station. Attracting a primarily male audience of 28- to 45-year-olds, The Fort plays classics from groups like the Eagles, Pink Floyd, and the Rolling Stones. On-air

radio personalities include Brian Casey, Matt Quinn, and Pat Thomas.

Listeners may know The Fort best as the host of the renowned *Bob and Tom in the Morning Show*, an Indianapolis-based talk show featuring the comic team of Bob Kevoian and Tom Griswold. Five days a week, listeners catch the latest jokes and pranks of this nationally syndicated program, which is also Fort Wayne's number one morning show. To demonstrate its support for the community, The Fort has donated more than $100,000 to local charities from the proceeds of Bob and Tom's many CDs.

WMEE 97.3 FM
WMEE is to the FM dial what WOWO is to the AM dial: a prominent radio station in the history of Fort Wayne. When it first aired in 1971, WMEE hit the airwaves as a Top 40 AM station. In 1979,

the station switched to FM and has been there ever since. WMEE, which targets a female audience of 18- to 34-year-olds, is famous for its promotions. In the past, it has given away a Corvette, organized and performed a human wave at Memorial Coliseum, and raised $103,000 for the Make-A-Wish Foundation during a 97-hour broadcast. "We try to do promotions that are bigger than life," Richards says.

On the heels of success in the 1980s with acts like Butcher and Richards in the mornings, WMEE struggled for a few years, trying to find its niche. After testing several different formats, the station settled on its current contemporary Top 40 format.

In 1996, during its 25th anniversary celebration, WMEE brought back all its past broadcasters, many of whom have gone on to bigger markets. That year also marked a rebirth of the station,

as WMEE's ratings jumped from 11th to fourth in the market.

WBYR 98.9 FM

When Fort Wayne wants rock, the city tunes to WBYR. Fondly called The Bear, WBYR caters to a male crowd aged 21 to 35 with its rock format. The station is anchored by Billy Elvis and Jack Hammer, who host *The Elvis and Hammer Show* every morning. This popular team released its first CD in 1998 and donated more than half the proceeds to Turnstone Center for Disabled Children and Adults. Throughout the day, listeners also enjoy the station's other popular DJs, Matt Talluto and Shannon Norris. Like WMEE, The Bear is well known for its promotions. Most Wednesdays during the summer, the station sponsors Bear in the Square at Freimann Square and serves free meals to the downtown lunch crowd. In the past, the event has served up to 600 people in a single lunch shift. For Christmas 1998, the Bear sponsored its first annual 17 Days of Christmas, a well-received promotion during which the station granted a different listener's Christmas wish each day for 17 days. Every January, WBYR also encourages listeners to donate blood by co-sponsoring the Bear Blood Drive in conjunction with the American Red Cross.

WQHK 105.1 FM

WQHK, also known as K105, is Federated Media's diamond station. Boasting personalities

like Dan Austin, BJ Stone, Rick Hughes, Jay Michaels, Mark Allen, Dude Walker, and Blair Garner, K105 has been ranked number one in Fort Wayne for three years running. Its format has attracted a loyal following of listeners who are passionate about country music.

The station attracts both women and men aged 18 to 49, and its programs are geared toward the whole family. To that end, K105 supports nearly anything related to the country lifestyle—from the music it plays to the many special programs and promotions it sponsors. On Saturday nights, for example, the station hosts a country dance party called *Boot Scootin' Party 'n' Nights* with Bo Reynolds. On Sunday nights, listeners can tune in to *American Country Countdown* with Bob Kingsley.

K105's promotions also focus on country music events. In the past, the station has sent listeners to Garth Brooks concerts and to events in Nashville. Locals have also become accustomed to hearing the moo of K105's Cash Cow year-round—whenever the cow moos, listeners can call in to win money.

Part of the station's success certainly lies in the interaction between its radio personalities and its listeners. K105 sends its DJs into the community regularly to conduct live broadcasts, and in 1998 alone, the station averaged almost five public appearances per week. "We like to meet people and just be out in the community," Richards says, adding that he wishes K105—and all the other stations in the Federated Media family—could know every listener by name.

WAYNE COMBUSTION SYSTEMS

ALTHOUGH MOST CONSUMERS DON'T REALIZE IT, WAYNE Combustion Systems manufactures products that are used in everyday living. "People don't realize how often they use our products," says General Manager Jeff Hoffman. Yet, for more than 70 years, Wayne Combustion Systems has made its presence known

around the world as a premier manufacturer of gas- and oil-fired burners commonly used in water heaters, furnaces, and gas ranges.

Wayne Combustion Systems works with a diverse group of clients around the world, but according to Hoffman, exports— excluding those to Canada—make up only about 3 percent of the business. Those exports are primarily distributed in Asia and in Central and South America.

In the oil burner industry, Wayne Combustion Systems supplies products for commercial and residential water heaters, boilers, and furnaces, as well as for unique applications such as deicing equipment and pressure washers. Its gas burners, on the other hand, are used in pizza ovens, bakers' ovens, steamers, and residential gas ranges. Wayne Combustion Systems also sells its burners to gas utility companies who use them when converting customers from oil to gas.

AN INDUSTRY LEADER

Wayne Combustion Systems was established in 1928 as Wayne Home Equipment, a manufacturer of oil burners used in oil-fired furnaces, boilers, and water heaters. In the 1940s, Wayne Home Equipment, seeking to diversify its product line, acquired Zepher Pump Company in Decatur, Illinois.

Perhaps one of the most significant changes to the company occurred in 1978, when Scott Fetzer purchased Wayne Home Equipment. Until that time, the Berghoff family of Fort Wayne had owned the firm.

Scott Fetzer is a subsidiary of Berkshire Hathaway, a $14 billion conglomerate controlled by Warren Buffett. Today, Scott Fetzer consists of 20 divisions,

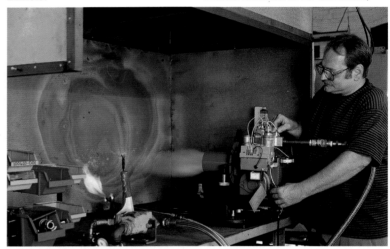

WAYNE COMBUSTION SYSTEMS HAS MADE ITS PRESENCE KNOWN AROUND THE WORLD AS A PREMIER MANUFAC- TURER OF GAS- AND OIL-FIRED BURNERS COMMONLY USED IN WATER HEATERS, FURNACES, AND GAS RANGES (TOP).

WAYNE COMBUSTION CREDITS ITS EMPLOYEES—SOME OF WHOM HAVE BEEN WITH THE COMPANY FOR MORE THAN 20 YEARS—WITH ITS HIGH MARKET RESPONSIVENESS (BOTTOM).

including Wayne Combustion Systems, which changed its name in 1998 to more accurately reflect its capabilities and its future direction. Becoming part of Scott Fetzer gave Wayne Combustion Systems the capital to grow and the ability to further enhance its strengths in the marketplace.

In 1980, the company introduced the Blue Angel oil burner, a high-efficiency burner that improves consumer appliance performance and is still the top-performing burner in the industry. Roughly 10 years later, the company moved the pump product line to a sister division in Ohio, cutting the number of employees in its headquarters from 400 to the current 70 who work in marketing, engineering, sales, manufacturing, and quality control.

In the oil burner side of the business, Hoffman says it's the ability to customize that has put Wayne Combustion Systems at the top. "We can customize any type of burner to fit a specific application," he says. The company's competition, on the other hand, simply mass-produces oil burners. Wayne Combustion Systems can also assist in developing a heat exchanger or combustion system.

For gas burners, Hoffman cites the company's combustion expertise as its main strength. Many of its employees have more than 20 years of experience in combustion-related work. For that reason, the company can solve a problem with a design in another system or provide a system that makes the customer's appliance more efficient.

TECHNOLOGY-ORIENTED SOLUTIONS

To stay ahead of its competition, Wayne Combustion Systems focuses on technology. "We want to develop technologies that keep us at the top and are able to be patented," Hoffman says. Throughout the years, the company has been awarded several patents, with more pending.

For example, Wayne Combustion Systems is working with several range manufacturers on a new, patented gas convection burner that provides more even cooking temperatures throughout the oven. This feature will be available on gas ranges in 2001.

Wayne Combustion Systems is also currently working on a design for a residential range that features low-profile gas burners. Rather than burners sitting on top of the gas range, these new burners will be enclosed in glass, thus making the range safer and more appealing.

NEW GROWTH

Wayne Combustion Systems currently occupies 196,000 square feet in a four-story, brick building. Working to increase its productivity, the company is taking steps to decrease manufacturing time from two weeks to three days, thus increasing its responsiveness to the marketplace.

Hoffman sees the company continuing to grow: "Currently, Wayne Combustion Systems is a $14 million company, and we want to be at $30 million in the next five years, honing in on the gas appliance market to perpetuate that growth."

As the sales of power burners increase dramatically, thanks to appliance manufacturers' working to meet new efficiency standards and environmental legislation, Wayne Combustion Systems will continue to grow. With its strong history, dedication to quality, and eye for technology, Wayne Combustion Systems will remain an industry leader for decades to come.

WAYNE COMBUSTION EMPLOYEES PERFORM A VARIETY OF TASKS IN SEVERAL IN-HOUSE DEPARTMENTS, INCLUDING (CLOCKWISE FROM TOP) THE DEVELOPMENT LABORATORY WHERE PRODUCTS SUCH AS COMMERCIAL DISHWASHERS ARE TESTED, THE OIL ASSEMBLY LINE, AND THE MACHINE SHOP WHERE EMPLOYEES CUT AIR TUBES.

FORT WAYNE
CITY *of* SPIRIT

▲ © BUD LEE

PHELPS DODGE MAGNET WIRE COMPANY

PHELPS DODGE MAGNET WIRE COMPANY BOASTS A long heritage of excellence in the magnet wire industry. Today, it is a recognized worldwide leader in developing magnet wire and wire coatings. ◆ The company originated in 1929 as the Inca Manufacturing Company. Its founding father was George Jacobs, the creator of the U.S. magnet wire industry and owner of Dudlo Manufacturing Company, which established Fort Wayne as the magnet wire center of the United States. After selling Dudlo, Jacobs started a new magnet wire company, which he called Inca Manufacturing. In 1931, he sold Inca to the Phelps Dodge Corporation, the world's second-largest producer of copper. Eventually, the company changed its name to Phelps Dodge Magnet Wire Company.

Today, Phelps Dodge Magnet Wire is the world's largest producer of magnet wire, the insulated conductor that lies at the heart of most electrical systems. Major markets for its products include motors, transformers, and coils for electrical and electronic equipment.

Worldwide, Phelps Dodge Magnet Wire employs 1,200 people, 440 of whom are located at the company's headquarters in Fort Wayne. In addition to its local facility, the company operates manufacturing facilities in Texas, North Carolina, and Mexico, as well as joint ventures in Kentucky and Austria. A sister company, Phelps Dodge International Corporation, also produces magnet wire from five locations in Latin America, the Pacific Rim, and Asia.

LEADER IN TECHNOLOGY

Phelps Dodge Magnet Wire operates under three basic principles. First is safety, which the company believes to be the single most important key for obtaining operational excellence. Environmental responsibility is the second principle by which the company works. Finally, Phelps Dodge Magnet Wire strives to provide customers the best-quality product.

However, it is Phelps Dodge Magnet Wire's tradition in technology that has truly bolstered its reputation as a world leader. The entrepreneurial spirit in the company has led to the invention of materials and insulation systems that are still used today throughout the magnet wire industry.

To strengthen its commitment to technology, Phelps Dodge Magnet Wire recently constructed a new facility in Fort Wayne, One Technology Center. The center includes state-of-the-art laboratories and pilot production facilities, which help maintain the company's reputation as a technology leader in the industry. Because of this focus, the company has been recognized by its customers around the world for the innovation and invention of electrical materials that are used to improve the products its customers make.

Phelps Dodge Magnet Wire has always been a loyal citizen of Fort Wayne, providing support to such projects as Headwaters Park, Embassy Theatre, and Science Central. It will go on serving the Fort Wayne area as it works to maintain and strengthen its position as a world leader and continue its tradition of pioneering the creation of value.

CLOCKWISE FROM TOP: LOCATED IN FORT WAYNE, PHELPS DODGE MAGNET WIRE COMPANY'S HEADQUARTERS IS THE SITE OF THE COMPANY'S TECHNOLOGY CENTER, WHICH CONTAINS STATE-OF-THE-ART LABORATORIES AND PILOT PRODUCTION FACILITIES FOR THE DEVELOPMENT, TESTING, AND EVALUATION OF NEW PRODUCTS AND PROCESS IMPROVEMENTS.

PHELPS DODGE MAGNET WIRE MAINTAINS A STRONG COMMITMENT TO RESEARCH AND DEVELOPMENT IN THE MAGNET WIRE INDUSTRY.

PHELPS DODGE MAGNET WIRE IS A RECOGNIZED LEADER IN DEVELOPING MAGNET WIRE COATINGS AND HOLDS MANY PATENTS ON MAGNET WIRE, ENAMELS, PACKAGES, AND EQUIPMENT. THE COMPANY ENGINEERS, MANUFACTURES, AND SELLS THE WORLD'S BROADEST LINE OF MAGNET WIRE, BARE CONDUCTORS, AND SPECIALTY PRODUCTS.

FORT WAYNE/ALLEN COUNTY CONVENTION AND VISITORS BUREAU

FORT WAYNE HAS MADE TREMENDOUS STRIDES IN BEcoming a major destination in the Midwest for conventions, trade shows, and leisure trips thanks to the efforts of the Fort Wayne/Allen County Convention and Visitors Bureau. Today, the Fort Wayne area hosts more than a million visitors annually for business meetings, conventions, leisure trips, and bus tours. Visitor spending adds more than $350 million to the local economy each year—helping to support more than 5,800 jobs in Allen County's tourism and hospitality industry.

The Convention and Visitors Bureau consists of 350 member businesses from both the private and the public sector. It is a coalition of convention facilities, attractions, museums, festivals, hotels, restaurants, and other businesses, all of which are committed to promoting Fort Wayne as the premier destination in the Midwest for both business meetings and leisure travel.

Says Convention and Visitors Bureau President Dan O'Connell, "The Bureau has grown from simply handing out city maps to being a dynamic marketing organization. We've enhanced our city's image and are now competing for large conventions that are attracting thousands of additional guests into our city. It's a total team effort that is making Fort Wayne a better place to live, work, and visit."

The Convention and Visitors Bureau welcomes the world to Fort Wayne. Through its Visitors Center, the Convention and Visitors Bureau showcases the community for visitors and offers guides, brochures, and travel assistance. Each year, the friendly staff at the Visitors Center answer more than 30,000 inquiries made by people from all over the world via phone, mail, E-mail, or walk-in guests.

FIND IT IN FORT WAYNE

The Convention and Visitors Bureau encourages visitors to Find It in Fort Wayne. Convention delegates, trade show attendees, and weekend visitors enjoy the wide variety and high quality of Fort Wayne's attractions, including the Fort Wayne Children's Zoo, the Foellinger-Freimann Botanical

Conservatory, and the Lincoln Museum. In addition, the Old City Hall Historical Museum, Museum of Art, Firefighters Museum, and Science Central are outstanding specialty attractions. The city is also home to the nation's second-largest genealogical collection at the Allen County Public Library, three professional minor-league sports teams, and numerous performing arts organizations offering entertainment options every week. There are also more than 10 cultural festivals for both visitors and residents to enjoy.

The Convention and Visitors Bureau markets Fort Wayne as an ideal location for conventions and shows seeking a central location in the Midwest. The Convention and Visitors Bureau promotes the Grand Wayne Center in downtown Fort Wayne for conventions, business meetings, and conferences, as well as the Allen County War Memorial Coliseum Exposition Center and Stadium as a superb space for arena events, trade shows, concerts, and sporting events. Fort Wayne's affordable hotels, numerous restaurants, and convenient transportation access by air or ground make the city a good choice for events with delegates from Indiana, Michigan, Illinois, and Ohio.

In the new millennium, the Convention and Visitors Bureau will continue to help the local economy grow by developing a strong, vibrant convention and tourism industry through its marketing and sales programs.

RACHEL KELLOGG

EACH YEAR, THE FRIENDLY STAFF AT THE FORT WAYNE CONVENTION AND VISITORS BUREAU'S VISITORS CENTER ANSWER MORE THAN 30,000 INQUIRIES MADE BY PEOPLE ALL OVER THE WORLD VIA PHONE, MAIL, E-MAIL, OR WALK-IN GUESTS.

PROMOTING FORT WAYNE AS THE CITY OF ATTRACTIONS, THE CONVENTION AND VISITORS BUREAU HIGHLIGHTS THE CITY'S MANY PARKS AND MUSEUMS, INCLUDING THE FORT WAYNE CHILDREN'S ZOO, THE FOELLINGER-FREIMANN BOTANICAL CONSERVATORY, AND THE LINCOLN MUSEUM.

CENTRAL SOYA COMPANY, INC.

THE GREAT DEPRESSION WAS GRIPPING THE COUNTRY when Dale W. McMillen started his own soybean-processing company. Although soybeans are an ancient crop, used first by the Chinese, it wasn't until 1904 that George Washington Carver discovered the soybean as a source of protein and oil. Few other people had recognized the value of soybeans. In fact, until then, they were used primarily for livestock forage. This key discovery has made the soybean an important major food source for the world.

McMillen's visionary insight helped create Central Soya Company, Inc., which today is a world leader in the research, development, and production of soy protein concentrates, lecithins, and other soybean products.

PIONEER OF TECHNOLOGY

McMillen founded Central Soya in 1934, locating the company's headquarters in Fort Wayne and its first plant in Decatur, Indiana. The company prospered as he pioneered the development of soybean processing and concentrate feed manufacturing through a division called McMillen Feed Mills. The feed was sold under its well-known trade name, Master Mix Feeds.

From its beginning, Central Soya earned a reputation as a pioneer of technology. In 1937, McMillen imported some of the first soybean extraction equipment to the United States. Four years later, the company issued its first patent for an extraction procedure that yielded a soybean meal rich in color and superior in nutritional quality.

In the 1950s, Central Soya added grain-merchandising operations and acquired the Chemurgy Division. Chemurgy added soy proteins and lecithins to the company's product line, and are now the leading components of Central Soya's value-added strategy.

In the 1960s, Central Soya began exporting soybean meal and livestock feed. A decade later, it built the company's first edible vegetable oil refinery in Decatur. To maintain its leadership position in the industry through new product research and development, the company also added a research and engineering facility in Fort Wayne.

From 1960 through 1985, Central Soya was a publicly traded company. That changed when a privately held company, owned by Roy Disney, Walt Disney's nephew, acquired Central Soya. Two years later, Central Soya was sold to its present owners, Paris-based Eridania Béghin-Say, a world leader in food ingredients and processed agricultural products with annual sales of approximately $12 billion. In

CENTRAL SOYA COMPANY, INC. HAS ALWAYS EMPHASIZED COMMUNITY INVOLVEMENT. IN 1962, FOUNDER DALE W. MCMILLEN, ALONG WITH MAJOR LEAGUE BALL PLAYER CARL ERSKINE, SUPPORTED THE LOCAL WILDCAT TIGER LEAGUE PLAYERS.

OPENED IN 1934, CENTRAL SOYA'S MULTIPURPOSE FACILITY IN DECATUR, INDIANA, WAS THE COMPANY'S FIRST PLANT, AS WELL AS THE FIRST EDIBLE VEGETABLE OIL REFINERY. TODAY, CENTRAL SOYA HAS GROWN INTO A LEADING MANUFACTURER OF FOODS AND FEED INGREDIENTS.

1994, Central Soya sold its feed business.

WORLD LEADER IN SOYBEAN PRODUCTS

Presently, Central Soya is a manufacturer of food and feed ingredients, with its single raw material being the soybean. From these soybeans come five products: soy meal, the main source of protein in animal diets; soy protein, which is used in a wide variety of prepared foods, processed meats, and specialized animal feeds; soy oil, an ingredient in salad oils, margarines, and bakery and snack foods, as well as industrial products; soy lecithins, a food ingredient and dietary supplement that promotes individual health; and isoflavones, dietary supplements to promote health.

The company has 12 operating facilities in the United States, including sites in Indiana, Illinois, Ohio, and Rhode Island, as well as two European manufacturing facilities, one in Denmark and the other in France. In the United States, office facilities are maintained in Fort Wayne; Washington, D.C.; and Chicago at the Board of Trade. International sales offices are located in Germany, China, and Brazil. Worldwide, the company employs nearly 1,300; in Indiana, it employs 670, which includes Fort Wayne headquarters.

Central Soya is a dominant leader in the eastern United States in its commodity business, which includes soybean meal and refined vegetable oil, and is a worldwide leader in the manufacturing of value-added products such as soybean protein and lecithin. This is all part of Central Soya's mission statement: being the best at adding value to agricultural products.

FOCUSED ON RESEARCH AND DEVELOPMENT

Throughout its history, Central Soya has committed its time and talent to research and development, one of the company's major strengths. Central Soya operates one of the leading research labs in the development of food products from soybeans. That focus on research and development has made the company a cutting-edge leader in food and feed technology.

RICH HERITAGE OF COMMUNITY SERVICE

Central Soya has always played a significant role in the communities where its facilities are located. In 1939, McMillen started a home-building project for the employees of Central Soya's Decatur plant. A year later, the program was begun in Gibson City, Illinois. Through the program, employees could acquire houses, which were built near the plants, at cost. In Decatur, 133 houses were built, while 40 homes were built in Gibson City.

Fort Wayne has also benefited from McMillen's generosity. In 1938, he donated 80 acres that became McMillen Park, now a thriving area with a pool, an indoor ice rink, an 18-hole golf course, tennis courts, ball diamonds, and picnic pavilions.

Then, in 1961, McMillen started Wildcat baseball in Fort Wayne as a league in which everybody makes the team and plays in every game. McMillen told his associates, "This is the greatest thing I ever did." This league has been a role model for other leagues around the country.

Today, this legacy of strong community service continues. Central Soya actively encourages employees to participate, through donations of time and money, in the communities in which employees live and work.

FUTURE IN FUNCTIONAL FOODS

With the Food and Drug Administration now heralding the exceptional nutritional value of soy, Central Soya is poised for a bright future. The company will continue its role in soybean processing and will focus on providing value-added soy products for the functional food market.

Functional foods address long-term health issues like heart health and osteoporosis. As functional foods play larger roles in the human diet, Central Soya will, no doubt, use its experience and expertise to make a positive impact on consumers' overall health.

CLOCKWISE FROM TOP LEFT: THE COMPANY OPERATES A STATE-OF-THE-ART, USDA-APPROVED RESEARCH LABORATORY FOR THE DEVELOPMENT OF FOOD PRODUCTS FROM SOYBEANS.

CENTRAL SOYA MANUFACTURES REFINED SOY OIL, WHICH IS THE WORLD'S MOST WIDELY CONSUMED EDIBLE VEGETABLE OIL.

CENTRAL SOYA IS POISED TO CAPITALIZE ON THE FUNCTIONAL FOOD MARKET WITH ITS LINE OF VALUE-ADDED SOY PROTEINS AND LECITHINS.

MidWest America Federal Credit Union

IdWest America Federal Credit Union's mission statement clearly illustrates its philosophy that its members come first: "committed to providing competitive, quality services for our members' financial success." ◆ A not-for-profit financial cooperative with a volunteer board of directors, MidWest America offers a full range of low-fee financial services for its members, including savings accounts, free checking, Visa credit card, mortgage lending, and safe-deposit boxes. One of the largest credit unions in Fort Wayne, MidWest America also offers convenience to its members with many ATMs located around the area—with more locations on the way.

MidWest America's senior management team includes Charles D. Bitler, president and CEO; Sallie Trimble, executive vice president; Michael Day, vice president, finance; Mary Fulkerson, vice president, lending; Cathy Schmidt, vice president, human resources; and Michael Woehnker, vice president, marketing and corporate communications.

Roots with General Electric

MidWest America got its start in 1936, when employees of General Electric (GE) petitioned to start a credit union. Chartered as General Electric Employees Federal Credit Union, this new financial institution originally occupied a small room inside the Fort Wayne GE plant. In the 1960s, the management bought land and built a permanent structure on Swinney Avenue, across from the plant.

Today, MidWest America's 160 employees serve members through 13 branches, including its headquarters on Medical Park Drive at North Clinton Street. Through mergers and growth, branches were established also in Illinois, Kentucky, and North Carolina.

To belong to the credit union, individuals must be eligible through one of the companies affiliated with MidWest America. In 1982, the credit union opened membership to employees from other affiliated companies. In 1987, the credit union changed its name to MidWest America to better reflect a diverse field of membership. Today, members can join by working for, or being related to, an employee of more than 350 companies, including Fort Wayne's three hospitals, the General Motors local plant, Fleetwood Motor Homes, and Scott's Food Stores. MidWest America has more than 60,000 members representing all 50 states.

Members enjoy benefits unique to MidWest America. Unlike most financial institutions, MidWest America insures savings accounts up to $350,000, as well as an additional $350,000 for IRA accounts. MidWest America also offers perks such as discount amusement park tickets,

CLOCKWISE FROM TOP: MIDWEST AMERICA FEDERAL CREDIT UNION'S HEADQUARTERS WAS BUILT IN 1987. BESIDES HAVING A BRANCH OFFICE ON THE FIRST FLOOR, THE BUILDING HOUSES SEVERAL SUPPORT DEPARTMENTS AND SENIOR MANAGEMENT ON THE SECOND FLOOR.

MIDWEST AMERICA HAS ENTERED A FLOAT IN THE FORT WAYNE THREE RIVERS FESTIVAL, A POPULAR EVENT EVERY JULY, EACH YEAR SINCE 1988, AND THE STAFF AND THEIR FAMILIES ENJOY WALKING ALONGSIDE THE FLOAT AS IT MAKES ITS WAY THROUGH THE HEART OF THE CITY.

MIDWEST AMERICA PROUDLY OPERATES MORE THAN 25 ATMS, CALLED STELLAR TELLERS. THE UNITS ARE PART OF THE MAC, NYCE, AND CIRRUS NETWORKS.

reduced-price movie tickets, and free notary service. Special clubs for children and older adults provide additional opportunities for members.

At the beginning of 1999, MidWest America introduced its Cowabunga Caffie Kids Club, which is open to children aged five to 12. The purpose of this club is to encourage kids to get in the habit of putting money into a savings account and to make it fun for them. Club members earn rewards for attaining various savings goals.

Even more popular is the Patriots Club for members who are more than 50 years old and meet minimum deposit requirements. More than 600 club members receive discounted financial services, free traveler's checks, and half-price safe-deposit boxes. They can also take advantage of special social opportunities, including day and overnight trips to destinations like Niagara Falls and a Mississippi riverboat cruise.

COMMUNITY INVOLVEMENT COMMITTEE

As a responsible member of the Fort Wayne community, MidWest America started a community involvement committee (CIC) to help support various charitable projects and nonprofit organizations. "The motto of credit unions is People Helping People, " says Woehnker. "We're not for profit, but for service."

The CIC's function is to raise money from among MidWest America's employees for worthwhile causes. Past fund-raising events have included dollar jeans days, selling entertainment books,

and holding bake sales and raffles. Money raised has been donated to organizations such as Make-A-Wish Foundation, Big Brothers/Big Sisters, Muscular Dystrophy Association (MDA), and St. Mary's Soup Kitchen. MidWest America also adopts several families at Christmas.

The response from employees has been overwhelming. "Our biggest reward is when we present the checks to organizations or meet the families we sponsor," Woehnker says, adding that employees say they get as much from the experience as the recipients of the donations.

ACCESSIBILITY AND FUTURE GROWTH

In order for its members to access its services more easily, in late 1996, MidWest America was one of the first credit unions in the area to put up a Web site. Internet banking was introduced in the summer of 1999. Located at www.mwafcu.org, the site pro-

vides information and services ranging from accessing personal accounts and transferring money to completing loan applications and calculating payments. "This is just another way our members can get in touch with us," Woehnker says.

MidWest America has a unique relationship with 14 current and former GE plants in Alabama, Arkansas, Florida, Illinois, Kentucky, Missouri, North Carolina, Tennessee, and Texas, whose employees have been doing business with MidWest America through payroll deductions and a toll-free number for 20 years. As its membership grows, the credit union is planning to add more branches and ATMs.

"MidWest America will always maintain its roots in Fort Wayne—that's our home," Woehnker says. With its long history of growth and success, MidWest America will continue to be a friendly place to do business in Fort Wayne for many years to come.

CLOCKWISE FROM TOP LEFT: EACH OF MIDWEST AMERICA'S BRANCH OFFICES CELEBRATED THE CREDIT UNION MEMBERSHIP ACCESS ACT SIGNED BY PRESIDENT BILL CLINTON WITH SPECIALLY DECORATED CAKES, BALLOONS, AND POSTERS. THE LAW RESTORED FEDERAL CREDIT UNIONS' ABILITY TO ADD NEW EMPLOYEE GROUPS.

THE SENIOR MANAGEMENT TEAM INCLUDES (FROM LEFT) MARY FULKERSON, VICE PRESIDENT, LENDING; CATHY SCHMIDT, VICE PRESIDENT, HUMAN RESOURCES; CHARLES D. BITLER, PRESIDENT AND CEO; SALLIE TRIMBLE, EXECUTIVE VICE PRESIDENT; MICHAEL DAY, VICE PRESIDENT, FINANCE; AND MIKE WOEHNKER, VICE PRESIDENT, MARKETING AND CORPORATE COMMUNICATIONS.

REGULAR VISITS TO MIDWEST AMERICA'S 350 SELECT EMPLOYEE GROUPS ARE SCHEDULED BY THE MARKETING DEPARTMENT TO INFORM THE ASSOCIATES OF NEW PRODUCTS AND SERVICES OF THE CREDIT UNION.

FORT WAYNE WIRE DIE, INC.

Of the country's 10 major diamond wire die manufacturers, more than half are headquartered in Fort Wayne, earning the city a reputation as the diamond wire die capital of the world. Nestled in the heart of this industry capital is Fort Wayne Wire Die, Inc., considered by many to be the grandfather of the wire die industry.

The Roots of an Industry

Fort Wayne Wire Die traces its roots back to the home of Paul Bieberich, who worked for the Dudlo Manufacturing Company in the 1920s. When Dudlo merged into what is today known as General Cable in 1932, Bieberich took the opportunity to become an independent die maker. He and three colleagues formed the Detroit Wire Die Company and operated out of Bieberich's basement until 1937, when Bieberich and a partner formed Fort Wayne Wire Die.

By 1939, the growth of the company into a 20-employee crew forced operations to move from Bieberich's basement to a garage. Three years later, Fort Wayne Wire Die built its own facility and, in 1975, after five expansions, moved to its current location near Fort Wayne International Airport.

Today, Fort Wayne Wire Die is the country's largest manufacturer of wire drawing dies, employing more than 300 associates. Still a family-owned company, the firm is currently operated by the second generation of Bieberichs—Dwight, Don, and their sister, Letha Scherer.

Using either single-crystal diamond, polycrystalline diamond, or tungsten carbide, the company produces wire drawing dies that range in size from one-tenth the diameter of a human hair (.0003 inch) to one-half inch in diameter.

Along with wire drawing dies, Fort Wayne Wire Die produces shaped profile dies, extrusion tips and dies, and other wear parts for the wire industry. The company also provides recutting and reconditioning services for diamond and carbide dies, and leads the industry in supplying new and recut matched elongation die sets for high-speed, multiwire drawing machines. Fort Wayne Wire Die also offers a full line of equipment for die reconditioning, inspection, and measurement.

Confronting Global Competition

In addition to its Fort Wayne headquarters, the company operates a manufacturing facility in London, Ontario, which was established as Advanced Wire Die Ltd. in 1947. Another manufacturing plant, acquired in 1960, is located in Columbus, North Carolina, and operates as Wayne Wire Die Co. In 1979, the firm opened Fortek GmbH, a sales office in Hofheim, Germany, to handle its European

sales. Agents and distributors in 35 countries now represent Fort Wayne Wire Die and its products.

Currently, the company exports its products to about 50 countries around the world. That number will inevitably grow as Fort Wayne Wire Die looks to expand its international presence. "This is a very competitive industry, especially when selling on a global basis," says International Marketing Manager Brad Scherer, grandson of founder Paul Bieberich. "One of our biggest challenges, and also our biggest focus in the future, is maintaining and building our international market share in a global economy."

KEYS TO SUCCESS

Being in the center of the diamond die capital of the world has certainly helped Fort Wayne Wire Die capture more business nationally and internationally. "When people in the industry think of Fort Wayne, they usually relate to Fort Wayne Wire Die," says Marketing Specialist Marianne Widenhofer, granddaughter of Paul Bieberich. The strong work ethic that characterizes the local population has also helped propel the company to the top of the industry, adds Widenhofer.

Undoubtedly, the factor that has contributed most to Fort Wayne Wire Die's success is the quality of its products. "People think quality when they think of Fort Wayne Wire Die," Scherer

says. The quality of the company's products reflects the high level of skill and productivity of its associates.

Along with superior product quality, Fort Wayne Wire Die's customers discover a company with the industry's largest sales and engineering staff, and the broadest range of products in the industry. Coupled with a wide array of high-tech equipment, most of which was designed and built by Fort Wayne Wire Die, those advantages give the company unparalleled capabilities, which it passes on to its customers in the form of top-quality products. In addition, Fort Wayne Wire Die is the first ISO 9002 registered wire die company in the United States.

"Our company also supports the educational development of our customers by conducting seminars and workshops focused

on providing them with the working knowledge, skill, and tools to succeed in their business," says Don Bieberich, vice president. More than 1,500 customers have attended these seminars and workshops.

A FAMILY APPROACH TO BUSINESS

Fort Wayne Wire Die takes special care to treat customers and employees as family. "Because we're a family-owned business, we're a little more paternalistic than other companies might be," Letha Scherer, secretary, says. "We try to take care of everybody." The company is obviously succeeding in doing just that. Many of its customers have worked with Fort Wayne Wire Die for more than 50 years. In addition, dozens of associates have been with the company for 25 or more years.

President Dwight Bieberich reflects on one of the basic foundations of the company: "It has always been an underlying principle through the years to build something of lasting value for both our customers and our family. Selling a top-quality product to our customers is a means of fulfilling our goals."

Longtime Fort Wayne Wire Die employees also remember the zest and drive of Paul Bieberich, who died in 1980. "He worked until he couldn't work anymore," says Brad Scherer, recalling his grandfather's unmistakable work ethic. "Most of the time, he was out on the production floor with his shirtsleeves rolled up and grease on his hands. That's just the way he preferred to work."

FORT WAYNE WIRE DIE OFFERS A FULL LINE OF EQUIPMENT FOR DIE RECONDITIONING, INSPECTION, AND MEASUREMENT.

TECHNICAL INNOVATION IS THE HALLMARK OF FORT WAYNE WIRE DIE, AND NOWHERE IS THAT MORE EVIDENT THAN IN THE DESIGN AND ENGINEERING DEPARTMENT. TOOLS SUCH AS THE THREE-DIMENSIONAL SOLID MODELING SOFTWARE ACCURATELY DEPICT THE PHYSICAL CHARACTERISTICS OF SPECIALLY DESIGNED DIES TO BE CERTAIN THEY SATISFY CUSTOMER REQUIREMENTS.

ICON International

ACCORDING TO RECENT STATISTICS, THE DESIGN AND production of exhibits for trade expositions, private events, and permanent installations such as museums, visitor centers, corporate showrooms, and TV news sets have been growing at double-digit rates for decades. Today, trade show expenditures

occupy the largest percentage of business-to-business marketing budgets. To ensure they obtain the most innovative solutions and product quality without compromise, organizations worldwide turn to Fort Wayne-based ICON International for their exhibits.

From modern, campuslike facilities, ICON's custom exhibit division, ICON Exhibits, designs, fabricates, transports, and services trade show requirements that range from lightweight, portable displays to huge, multistory exhibits that can be assembled and reconfigured in a matter of hours using the latest exhibit systems technology. In 1999, ICON handled more than 2,000 such events for

clients throughout the world. For its national sales convention, one client called on ICON to produce a replica of a typical American small town, a project requiring more than 100,000 square feet of exhibitry. Another client asked ICON to create small, glass-encased displays of Abraham Lincoln's folded hands for use as prestigious gifts, an example of the company's workmanship.

In the realm of museums and environments, ICON Exhibits has collaborated with world-class designers to produce exhibits for museums, and has been recognized for its work on the Lincoln and John Dillinger museums in Indiana. The company has designed numerous corporate lobbies, showrooms, and visitor centers, and has developed interactive exhibits for schools and science museums.

ONE-OF-A-KIND PRODUCTS

ICON has its roots in Customcraft, a company founded in Fort Wayne 1946 to build everything from gun turrets for aircraft to custom furniture for the homes of renowned architect Frank Lloyd Wright. As its reputation for quality craftsmanship grew, so too did the scope of its projects. Soon, Customcraft earned recognition as a one-of-a-kind innovator, a trait that made it an ideal

enterprise for the design and production of custom exhibits for trade shows and museums.

In 1979, Michael V. Parrott acquired Customcraft from its original owners, renamed it ICON Exhibits, and directed its efforts into the kind of exhibitions and innovations that would mark the company as a strong, creative force in the industry. In 1981, ICON Exhibits introduced its first major contribution to the trade show industry: ExhibitPak, the first self-contained exhibit. Nine years later, ICON unveiled a unique, proprietary, structural exhibit system called ExZact, which featured modular construction that allowed it to be reconfigured as much as needed. ExZact was followed by the revolutionary ExpoDeck in 1996, a lightweight, aluminum structural system that can also be reconfigured for different multidecking applications.

These innovations led ICON to open other divisions. In 1984, it started Displaysource, which specializes in lightweight, portable displays and has showrooms located in Indianapolis and Fort Wayne. In 1998, a division called Highmark Technologies opened in Indianapolis to manage ICON's proprietary high-performance exhibit systems products. Today, Highmark Technologies develops, designs, and installs multilevel

ICON INTERNATIONAL IS STRATEGICALLY LOCATED IN FORT WAYNE, WHICH IS WITHIN A ONE-DAY DRIVE OF MORE THAN 75 PERCENT OF ALL TRADE SHOWS (LEFT).

ICON EXHIBITS HAS RECEIVED NUMEROUS AWARDS FOR ITS GROUNDBREAKING DESIGNS, INCLUDING THE INTERNATIONAL EXHIBITORS ASSOCIATION'S 1996 GRAND AWARD FOR ITS MAGNAVOX EXHIBIT (RIGHT).

ICON PRODUCES A WIDE VARIETY OF EXHIBITS FOR NUMEROUS HIGH-PROFILE CLIENTS, INCLUDING (CLOCKWISE FROM TOP LEFT) A CORPORATE TRADESHOW EXHIBIT FOR AMERITECH, AN ADVANCED TECHNOLOGIES EXHIBIT FOR ICON, A CORPORATE ENVIRONMENT EXHIBIT FOR GRANGE INSURANCE, AND A MUSEUM EXHIBIT FOR THE LINCOLN MUSEUM.

exhibits, as well as sells Expo-Deck to other exhibit builders around the world. To reflect its global presence, ICON officially became known as ICON International in 1998.

STRATEGIC LOCATION AND SUPERIOR PRODUCTS

Most of ICON's competitors are based in major metropolitan areas, so it might seem a little unusual for it to be headquartered in a smaller community like Fort Wayne. But Parrott says Fort Wayne is strategically located within a one-day drive of more than 75 percent of all trade shows, reducing exhibit transport costs and delivery times. In addition, the city boasts distinct cost advantages over other communities. "With our innovative designs and unique products, coupled with the cost and transportation advantages of doing business in Fort Wayne," Parrott says, "we provide unmatched value for our clients no matter where they are located."

But as Parrott notes, low cost is only one benefit companies receive in working with ICON.

Other advantages include full-service design, production, graphics, event support, and exhibit property management services at world-class levels. Businesses not wishing to invest in their own exhibit properties can still turn to ICON for a wide selection of rental systems and accessories.

ICON lends its years of trade show expertise and design creativity to every project. "We understand the most creative and cost-effective use of a systems approach to trade show exhibiting," Parrott says, "and we use the latest materials and lighting techniques, along with the most exciting graphics to create memorable messages." Such excellence is obvious from the numerous awards ICON and its clients have received at trade shows, including dozens of Best of Show honors. In 1996, for example, an ICON-designed and -built double-deck exhibit for a multinational electronics company won the top award from the International Exhibitors Association. A year later, the same exhibit properties

were transformed into another award-winning exhibition.

BENCHMARK OF EXHIBITING EXCELLENCE

One of the challenges facing ICON concerns supporting clients globally. The company employs skilled project managers who coordinate every aspect of a trade event, which gets tougher as its clients move increasingly into the international arena. To accomplish this, the company is equipped with the best systems products and the latest computer-based data storage, communication, and design technology to enable instantaneous linkage to clients around the globe.

For ICON, which boasts a solid past, the future looks even brighter. Parrott anticipates opening satellite offices on the East and West coasts, perhaps one day overseas. Geographic growth will match the growth inside the company as ICON works to achieve a position as "America's benchmark of exhibiting excellence," a feat it is well on its way to accomplishing.

DON R. FRUCHEY, INC.

P

ON FRUCHEY HAD MINIMAL FINANCIAL RESOURCES WHEN he founded his company, but his determination and his ability to attract highly skilled people built Don R. Fruchey, Inc. into one of the largest specialty contractors in the Midwest. ◆ Fruchey established the company in May 1950. His original vision

was to be a small but successful steel erection contractor. "Our goal was to be one of the best, not one of the biggest, companies between Chicago and Cleveland," says Fruchey, who retired in 1980. Over the years, however, the company grew much more than he had anticipated.

During the early part of its history, steel and precast concrete erection for new buildings and bridges was a major focus. In the 1960s, Don R. Fruchey, Inc. erected the 3,606-foot-long Interstate 75 Expressway Bridge in Toledo, Ohio, and the Riverfront Stadium in Cincinnati. Back home in Fort Wayne, the company erected the City-County Building, the public library, and the recent South Side High School expansion.

The company's vision shifted as it grew. Eventually, industrial

AS A COST-SAVING MEASURE FOR A CUSTOMER, WHEN THIS STRUCTURAL STEEL FOR A NEW FOUNDRY WAS ERECTED, DON R. FRUCHEY, INC. INSTALLED THE EQUIPMENT DURING THE STEEL-ERECTION PROCESS. IN ADDITION, THE COMPANY INSTALLED ALL OF THE REMAINING EQUIPMENT IN THE PLANT (TOP).

"OUR GOAL WAS TO BE ONE OF THE BEST, NOT ONE OF THE BIGGEST, COMPANIES BETWEEN CHICAGO AND CLEVELAND," SAYS FOUNDER DON FRUCHEY (BOTTOM).

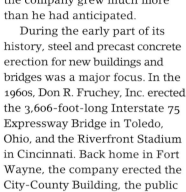

equipment installation and plant maintenance services became the backbone of the company.

Fruchey's sons, Robert and David, now run the company as president and vice president, respectively. His daughter, Donna Baughman, also works for the company, which is headquartered in a renovated, historic inn that once served travelers on the Wabash-Erie Canal.

DIVERSIFIED INDUSTRIAL SERVICES

Don R. Fruchey, Inc. is a single-source supplier for its customers, who are located mainly in the Midwest, although projects take place across the country. Its industrial services are diversified to meet customer needs. These include equipment installation, steel construction, custom steel fabrication, specialized hauling, and equipment warehousing.

Don R. Fruchey, Inc. installs equipment for all industry types and sizes, from foundries to auto assembly to food processing. This work can demand high levels of precision skill and knowledge. An equipment installation can mean installing just one machine or moving an entire industrial facility. In one unique project, the company dismantled and reinstalled an entire foundry from California to Arkansas, including 96 truckloads of equipment.

The company's steel construction projects involve new building construction, as well as modifications to existing buildings. Recent projects include Auburn Foundry's Plant II, Chase Brass and Copper's plant addition, and the Box Washer addition at General Motors Truck and Bus.

PWC Fabrication, a division of Don R. Fruchey, Inc., offers a modern shop, a broad range of equipment, and a team of skilled fabricators. It fabricates everything from structural steel to industrial furnaces to complicated conveyor systems.

Industrial equipment has become increasingly sophisticated and expensive over the years. To transport it, Don R. Fruchey, Inc. has a team of dedicated drivers and a fleet of specialized tractors and trailers, most of which have air-ride suspensions.

In addition, the company's warehousing facilities can act as a holding area for equipment awaiting installation or final disposition plans. Crating and equipment modification can be provided. Warehousing facilities currently consist of 75,000 square feet on-site and 140,000 square feet of third-party space.

EMPLOYEE LOYALTY

Because the work it performs is so specialized, Don R. Fruchey, Inc. relies on a highly skilled team of employees. Robert Fruchey believes its employees set the company apart: "Their sophistication and their knowledge of the type of work we do are unparalleled in the industry." That is a crucial component for success in an industry where clients are trimming engineering support. "For example," he continues, "our field forces must increasingly make on-site decisions to keep projects on schedule."

Typically, Don R. Fruchey, Inc. maintains an employee base of 120 to 150 people. That number fluctuates, depending on the current number of projects. One consistent element that speaks volumes is employee loyalty to the company. "We have three generations of families working here," says Don Fruchey.

Employees take pride in the equipment that also defines Don R. Fruchey, Inc. The company maintains a fleet of equipment and tools that can meet nearly every need. This includes everything from hydraulic gantries to precision leveling/alignment tools to a computer-controlled burning table at PWC. "We have an excellent maintenance facility to supply our craftsmen and customers with safe, dependable equipment," David Fruchey says.

A MORE TECHNICAL FUTURE

As Robert Fruchey looks to the future, he envisions more growth for the company, as it forms relationships with new customers. He also anticipates offering even more technical and computer support from all areas of the company, as well as more training to keep employees current with advancing technologies.

BUILDING ON SUCCESS

In 2000, Don R. Fruchey, Inc. celebrates its 50th anniversary. While the company will honor past achievements, the focus will remain on the goals that have served it well for 50 years. Excellent customer service and solid employment for its people will continue to be the foundations for a prosperous future.

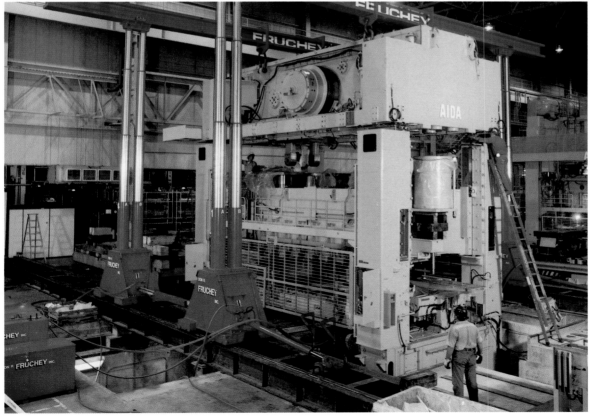

CLOCKWISE FROM LEFT: PWC FABRICATION, A DIVISION OF DON R. FRUCHEY, INC., FABRICATES 925 FEET OF HEAVY DUCT SECTIONS.

A DON R. FRUCHEY, INC. DRIVER PREPARES A SECTION OF PWC FABRICATION DUCTWORK FOR SHIPMENT. USING ITS OWN TRACTORS AND SPECIALTY TRAILERS FOR THIS SINGLE-SOURCE PROJECT, DON R. FRUCHEY, INC. TRANSPORTED AND INSTALLED THE DUCTWORK AT THE CUSTOMER SITE.

A 231,000-POUND CROWN FOR A STAMPING PRESS IS SET WITH ONE OF DON R. FRUCHEY, INC.'S HYDRAULIC GANTRY SYSTEMS.

ELLISON BAKERY INC.

MOUTHWATERING SMELLS OF HOMEMADE COOKIES WAFT through the air at Ellison Bakery Inc., reminders of the freshness and quality that have made cookies from this Indiana mainstay some of the best in the country. In 2000, Ellison Bakery celebrated 50 years of producing its trademark, melt-in-your-mouth cookies.

THE BIRTH OF A BAKERY

In 1945, Donald Ellis started a doughnut shop in his family's two-car garage in Fort Wayne. Eventually, the business grew to include pies, pastries, and other sweets. His siblings joined in to assist him in the process; in fact, his brother William, now chairman of the board for Ellison Bakery, was his top cookie maker.

As the business continued to grow, so too did the need for a new location. In 1948, the bakery moved to a site it named Ellisville on U.S. 24, where the family also opened a service station, grocery store, restaurant, and garage, and eventually added a motel. One year later, in the days when a dozen cookies sold for just 29 cents, Donald Ellis accepted a license to produce Swanson Homemade Cookies. That venture later became known as Archway Cookies. In 1950, Donald Ellis and his family officially incorporated as Ellison Bakery.

For more than a decade, Ellison Bakery was the official Archway licensee for all of Indiana and Kentucky. With the addition of Wisconsin to its territory in 1963, the company was forced to relocate to larger quarters, so in 1965, it constructed a plant across the street from the Fort Wayne International Airport. Baking at the new site began in December of that year.

In the early 1980s, along with supplying roughly 50 varieties of cookies for Archway, Ellison Bakery began servicing the institutional, fund-raising, and ice-cream industries. In 1997, the company made a first-of-a-kind agreement with Archway. Rather than working as a licensee for only three states, Ellison Bakery agreed to supply certain varieties of Archway products throughout the country.

COOKIES BY THE MILLION DOZEN

Today, Ellison Bakery is owned by Chairman of the Board William

Ellis, President Robert Ellis Jr., and Vice President Richard Smith. Under their leadership, the company continues to supply roughly 14 varieties of cookies for Archway. Ellison Bakery also provides cookies and crunches to the ice-cream industry—and makes cookies for various institutions, including schools, nursing homes, and hospitals. Since the 1980s, the company's annual tonnage volume has doubled, with 1999 showing the highest volume in sales in Ellison's history.

To put the growing operation in perspective, Ellison Bakery uses 4,000 to 5,000 pounds of dough an hour between two band ovens (one being 150 feet long). That makes two to three batches of cookies every hour, with one batch totaling 2,000 dozen one-ounce cookies. The average cookie takes eight minutes to go through the oven. After a full day, Ellison Bakery produces about 100,000 dozen one-ounce cookies—that's 30 million dozen one-ounce cookies a year.

IN 2000, ELLISON BAKERY INC. CELEBRATED 50 YEARS OF PRODUCING ITS TRADEMARK, MELT-IN-YOUR-MOUTH COOKIES.

What makes cookies from Ellison Bakery unique is their softness. Although some of its cookies, like those made into crunches for the ice-cream industry, do have a harder, crunchier texture, most of its products are soft, home-style cookies. Additionally, most varieties from Ellison Bakery have short shelf lives, which means they have no preservatives.

In recent years, the company has also faced the cries of consumers who were demanding low-fat and sometimes no-fat products. Archway's cookies, however, have always been lower in fat than many other brands. Although the fat-conscious pleas have quieted, there is now a small but significant demand for sugar-free cookies. Ellison Bakery currently produces a number of sugar-free products to serve this small niche market.

But regardless of the ever changing consumer market, William Ellis says, "We've always tried to produce the best cookie we can." That philosophy has been instilled in the company's 80 employees, many of whom have worked for Ellison Bakery for 25, 30, and even 40 years.

Meeting the Challenges of Growth

As growth in the market continues, Ellison Bakery will continue to address its own expansion needs. When employees retire or when an increase in business requires temporary help, finding employees to fill those spots is sometimes difficult in Fort Wayne, a community with a very low unemployment rate. "We're trying to reach and service the whole nation, but because of our size, it's not always easy," says Robert Ellis Jr., adding that General Manager Todd Wallin is helping to overcome these challenges.

Ellison Bakery is also looking to expand the size of its ovens, once again increasing its output. In fact, the company is already considering adding another 50 feet to one of the ovens if growth continues at its current rate. According to Robert Ellis Jr., the trick is to avoid growing too quickly. "We want to be sure business will be there before we go the next step," he says. "We've always had conservative growth, and we'll continue taking it slowly."

But the company's cautious business philosophy doesn't mean Ellison Bakery will slow down on making some of the best-tasting cookies on both sides of the Mississippi. That's just the way the cookie doesn't crumble.

ELLISON BAKERY IS A FAMILY-OWNED BUSINESS, LED BY (FROM LEFT) ROBERT ELLIS JR., PRESIDENT; RICHARD SMITH, VICE PRESIDENT; AND WILLIAM ELLIS, CHAIRMAN OF THE BOARD.

AFTER A FULL DAY, ELLISON BAKERY PRODUCES ABOUT 100,000 DOZEN ONE-OUNCE COOKIES—THAT'S 30 MILLION DOZEN ONE-OUNCE COOKIES A YEAR.

FORT WAYNE RADIOLOGY

FORT WAYNE RADIOLOGY BOASTS A HISTORY OF FIRSTS. Not only was it the first radiology group in Fort Wayne, it was the first to introduce previously unavailable, high-tech services to the area. "Fort Wayne Radiology has been a leader in Northeast Indiana since its beginning," says Karen Rothermund,

director of marketing and community relations. Fort Wayne Radiology's accomplishments reflect its desire to provide the highest-quality health care to its patients.

Founded in 1950 by Dr. J.L. Loudermilk, Fort Wayne Radiology provides full-service radiology needs to patients in Indiana, Ohio, and Michigan. Its current staff consists of 23 board-certified, highly trained physicians and 70 support personnel, all of whom collectively performed more than 200,000 procedures in 1998. The association's radiologists have specialties in several areas, including skeletal radiology, magnetic resonance imaging (MRI),

abdominal imaging, diagnostic radiology, computed tomography (CT), vascular and interventional radiology, and body imaging. The group produces a quarterly newsletter directed to physicians that provides advancements in technologies and diagnostic procedures.

A HALF-CENTURY OF FIRSTS
In 1950, Fort Wayne Radiology became the first Fort Wayne group practice to provide services to outlying hospitals. Today, it is associated with more than 14 radiology facilities, including Parkview Memorial Hospital, where it provides 24-hour coverage; Whitley County Hospital; Huntington Memorial Hospital; Wabash County Hospital; and Cameron Hospital. These radiology centers service outlying areas through innovative technologies, such as teleradiology, which provides 24-hour radiology coverage to remote facilities via a sophisticated computer network system (PACS).

Other advancements in technology include dual-energy X-ray absorptiometry (DEXA), a bone mineral analysis test to detect osteoporosis. Current studies indicate that osteoporosis in the United States affects more than 20 million women and 5 million men, most of whom are

over the age of 50. To fight this disease, Fort Wayne Radiology in 1996 established DEXA Diagnostics, a mobile service that was the first equipment of its kind in the Fort Wayne area. The mobile service performs approximately 220 bone mineral analyses each month.

In 1975, Fort Wayne Radiology introduced the first total body CT scanner in the state of Indiana. Just 10 years later, radiologists in the practice established the first MRI scanner in Northeast Indiana. Those achievements were followed in 1989 by the founding of the Breast Diagnostic Center. Located in Carew Medical Park with a screening center at Woodland Plaza, the Breast Diagnostic Center is dedicated to performing mammograms and addressing breast issues and wellness. Since it opened, the Breast Diagnostic Center has performed more than 90,000 mammograms. Staff radiologists are on-site to answer questions and interpret test results. The center, which is accredited by the American College of Radiology (ACR), also produces a biannual newsletter to keep patients informed of relevant information and technologies. In 1997, the Breast Diagnostic Center added another first of its kind in the area: Advanced Breast Biopsy Instrumentation (ABBI),

FORT WAYNE RADIOLOGY PROVIDES FULL-SERVICE RADIOLOGY NEEDS TO PATIENTS IN INDIANA, OHIO, AND MICHIGAN. ITS CURRENT STAFF CONSISTS OF 23 BOARD-CERTIFIED, HIGHLY TRAINED PHYSICIANS AND 70 SUPPORT PERSONNEL, ALL OF WHOM COLLECTIVELY PERFORMED MORE THAN 200,000 PROCEDURES IN 1998.

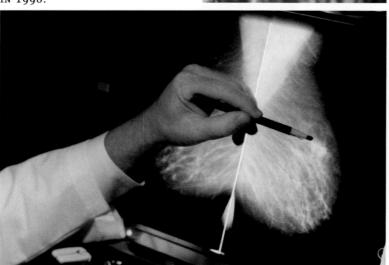

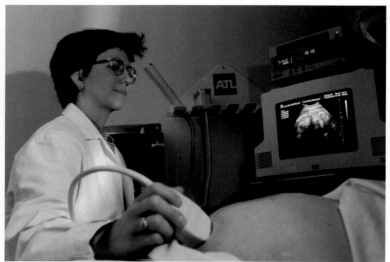

which allows for faster recovery time after a biopsy.

Later that same year, Fort Wayne Radiology brought specialized imaging to Northeast Indiana with Open View MRI in Parkwest Center. This new technology eliminates anxiety and discomfort when performing an MRI. In 1998, Fort Wayne Radiology's MRI Center became the first MRI facility in Indiana to be accredited by the American College of Radiology. Of the 1,600 applicants nationwide, fewer than 20 achieved this prestigious status.

To continue expanding and improving its services, Fort Wayne Radiology joined seven other radiology groups in 1996 to form the Indiana Imaging Network. More than 100 radiologists from Bloomington, Columbus, Evansville, Fort Wayne, Muncie, South Bend, and West Terre Haute make up the network. Through this association with doctors around the state, Fort Wayne Radiology can further its expertise and negotiate statewide contracts with large employers and patient groups.

A Web site developed in 1998 has allowed Fort Wayne Radiology to expand its services for its patients. "We designed the site as a patient resource," Rothermund says. The site— www.fwradiology.com—provides

updates on health issues, as well as links to medical societies and associations.

John Reed, M.D., president of Fort Wayne Radiology Association, says this drive to excel separates the organization from other practices like it. "Our commitment to excellence and new technology defines who we are and what we do," he says. "We're always working in the best interest of our patients."

Making Strides for the Community

Fort Wayne Radiology has played a large role in the Fort Wayne community. It has participated in Focus on Health for more than five years, setting up booths at the regularly scheduled health fairs to educate the public about osteoporosis, breast cancer, and other health issues. Fort Wayne Radiology also donates its services to not-for-profit organizations,

such as Matthew 25 and other community health-related programs.

In addition, in 1998, Fort Wayne Radiology cosponsored the first annual Making Strides Against Breast Cancer, a five-mile walk to raise money for the American Cancer Society. In the first year of the event, more than 1,000 men, women, and children participated, raising in excess of $75,000.

Plans for Fort Wayne Radiology's future are based on its founding philosophy of providing high-quality health care to the Fort Wayne community. By continuing to strengthen its services, provide the latest technology, and advance the capabilities of diagnostic medicine to the highest level, Fort Wayne Radiology's future will continue to set the standards and remain the leader in radiology services for Northeast Indiana.

MAGNETIC RESONANCE IMAGING (MRI) REPRESENTS A breakthrough in medical technology. It creates detailed images that allow physicians to look inside a person's body, a process the Fort Wayne Radiology MRI Center has perfected. ◆ Advanced Imaging Systems, Inc., dba the Fort Wayne Radiology MRI Center—which is an affiliate of the Fort Wayne Radiology Association—was founded in 1985 to provide leading-edge, diagnostic MRI studies to patients and physicians. In 1998, the MRI Center became Indiana's first MRI facility to be accredited by the American College of Radiology. Of the 1,600 applicants for accreditation, fewer than 20 were awarded this status. Today, the MRI Center provides magnetic resonance imaging services to patients who are primarily from Fort Wayne and the surrounding areas. The center also receives referrals from physicians in southern Michigan and western Ohio.

HIGHLY TRAINED PROFESSIONALS

The physicians at the MRI Center are highly trained professionals. The 15-member staff consists of MRI-trained technologists and radiologists who are fellowship-trained MRI and neuroradiology specialists, all of whom have been with the MRI Center for years. This fact speaks highly of the center's capabilities. Kelly Ferrell, M.D., director of the MRI Center, says, "Their longevity says a great deal about their competence and their satisfaction on the job, which translates into how they care for patients."

Patient safety is a high priority at the center. Unlike other, similar facilities, the nurses at the MRI Center all hold the American Cardiac Life Support certificate, which is usually required in emergency rooms, but not in outpatient centers like the MRI Center. Finding nurses with this certification can be challenging, but the center knows it is well worth the effort. "Because we're working for our patients," Ferrell says, "we're going to do everything we can to increase their safety."

The MRI Center uses the most technologically advanced equipment available. For example, according to Ferrell, the center is currently the only site with imaging capabilities to perform early analysis of stroke detection. "We have an ongoing policy of upgrading our software and our hardware to stay at the leading edge of technology in northern Indiana," he says. In addition, the MRI Center uses a unique digital image transmission that allows for precise readings. Ferrell explains the quality as the difference between listening to music on a compact disc and on a cassette tape.

In the future, the MRI Center hopes to be the leader in using MRI scanning for different areas of the body. Currently, for example, scans of the abdomen and chest are performed by technologies other than MRI. Says Ferrell, "We hope we can demonstrate the superiority of magnetic resonance imaging in those areas in the years ahead."

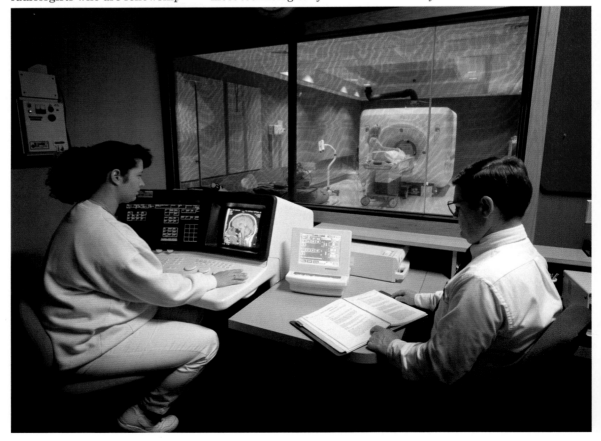

A BREAKTHROUGH IN MEDICAL TECHNOLOGY, MAGNETIC RESONANCE IMAGING (MRI) ALLOWS PHYSICIANS TO LOOK INSIDE A PERSON'S BODY. IT IS A PROCESS THE FORT WAYNE RADIOLOGY MRI CENTER, AN AFFILIATE OF FORT WAYNE RADIOLOGY ASSOCIATION, HAS MASTERED.

OPEN VIEW MRI REPRESENTS A UNIQUE CONCEPT IN medical imaging in the Fort Wayne area. Not only does the center offer state-of-the-art technology, its location in a shopping area provides a unique, nonthreatening environment. ◆ Open View MRI is located in Parkwest Shopping Center on the south-

west side of Fort Wayne. Its patients experience an environment completely unlike that of a hospital or medical center. "We wanted to eliminate the anxiety typically associated with a hospital experience," says Thomas Sarosi, M.D., a neuroradiologist and technical director at Open View MRI. The center's location was chosen for its visibility to passersby and its proximity to shopping areas. Patients can fit their appointments in while running errands; for convenience, the center offers evening and weekend appointments.

AREA'S FIRST OPEN VIEW TECHNOLOGY

Fort Wayne Radiology introduced Open View MRI in 1997 as the first center of its kind in the Fort Wayne area. In spring 2000, Open View MRI was accredited by the American College of Radiology. To date, only 14 MRI facilities in the state of Indiana have earned the prestigious three-year certification. Prior to this, a special needs patient who required magnetic resonance imaging (MRI) had to

endure the discomfort of conventional MRI systems. Those systems, which are enclosed, were particularly uncomfortable for claustrophobic or larger patients. In fact, according to Sarosi, claustrophobic patients who couldn't tolerate the enclosure often had to be turned away or sedated.

State-of-the-art equipment features an extra-large opening that allows airflow and an open view around a patient's body, thus eliminating feelings of claustrophobia or discomfort. "This equipment is much more comfortable for many patients," Sarosi says. "In fact, we rarely have problems."

Children are also good candidates for open view imaging. Because of the open design of the equipment, parents or other caregivers can hold a frightened child's hand and offer comfort without interfering with the quality of the scan.

COMFORTING ENVIRONMENT

The center resembles a private doctor's office, complete with

televisions and comfortable sofas. The eight staff members go out of their way to ensure patient ease. "We try to make everybody feel calm and comfortable," Sarosi says. "For many of our patients, we take the time to walk them around the equipment and have them lie under the equipment until they feel comfortable enough to proceed."

Most of Open View MRI's patients come from physician referrals. Because of its uniqueness, Open View MRI attracts patients from elsewhere throughout Indiana, as well as Ohio and Michigan. In addition, the center also services the diagnostic needs of the Fort Wayne Fury, the city's CBA basketball team.

Since its opening, Open View MRI has been well received by patients and physicians. "There was a demand for this type of technology," Sarosi says, "and we filled it." He adds that patients are so pleased with Open View MRI, they often say they'll never go anywhere else for an MRI.

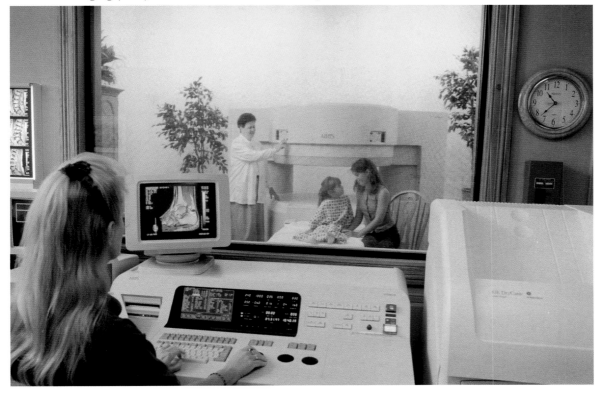

CHILDREN ARE GOOD CANDIDATES FOR OPEN VIEW MRI IMAGING. BECAUSE OF THE OPEN DESIGN OF THE EQUIPMENT, PARENTS OR OTHER CAREGIVERS CAN HOLD A FRIGHTENED CHILD'S HAND AND OFFER COMFORT WITHOUT INTERFERING WITH THE QUALITY OF THE SCAN.

PHD, Inc.

PROVIDE THE CUSTOMERS WHAT THEY WANT, WHEN THEY want it." This is the essence of what PHD, Inc. does to ensure its position as a leader in the industrial automation industry. ◆ In 1957, PHD began its successful journey under the name Pneumatic Hydraulic Development Company. One of the company's

first products, Tom Thumb® Cylinders, quickly became a dominant player in the industrial automation industry. As the need for automated manufacturing processes grew, so did the company's product line. In 1976, the company officially became known as PHD, Inc.

Today, the company designs and manufactures an extensive line of pneumatic, hydraulic, and electromechanical components that can be used independently or combined in a modular configuration for cost-effective automation solutions. The modularity concept began in the early 1980s, when PHD was the only company working with modular automation. As the concept's popularity increased, so did the number of companies using this innovative method. "It's an indication that the market has

matured," says Walt Hessler, vice president of sales and marketing.

PHD's success came about from its progressive approach to the development and designing of new products. The company's dynamic automation experts use the latest technology and state-of-the-art engineering to create products of the future.

LEADING THE INDUSTRY

For several decades, PHD has dominated the industrial automation market. The company's extensive range of products, unique options, and made-to-order manufacturing processes set it apart from the industry's traditional commodity manufacturers. Known for ruggedness, precise positioning, and extremely long life, PHD's products have all the quality and performance that design engineers demand. In addition, PHD's engineering and manufacturing processes are quality system certified under their current ISO-9002 certification.

Currently, the $45 million company employs more than 400 people. PHD has operations in three facilities in Fort Wayne, including a new, 80,000-square-

foot, state-of-the-art manufacturing plant. Other locations include one facility in Huntington, Indiana; a branch office in Germany (PHD GmbH); and another branch office in England (PHD Ltd.). Products are sold nationally and abroad by PHD's exclusive network of specially trained distributors. Considered technical salespeople by trade, PHD distributors don't simply take orders; they meet with customers to determine their needs and then recommend the best solutions to meet those challenges. This worldwide distributor network has become an extension of PHD's commitment to provide excellent customer service at the local level internationally.

Another contributor to PHD's success is its Custom Products Team. For more than 30 years, the company has designed and manufactured custom products to fit unique application requirements. This talented group welcomes and encourages requests for specialized products, regardless of quantity or ordering frequency.

PHD DELIVERS

In today's fast-paced, competitive markets, PHD's employees

PHD, INC.'S COMPLETE LINE OF ENGINEERING SOFTWARE ENABLES CUSTOMERS TO QUICKLY SPECIFY, SELECT, AND DESIGN PRODUCTS TO FIT THEIR INDIVIDUAL AUTOMATION NEEDS (RIGHT).

PHD ACTUATORS CAN BE EASILY COMBINED TO FORM SIMPLE PICK-AND-PLACE SOLUTIONS FOR INDUSTRIAL AUTOMATION (LEFT).

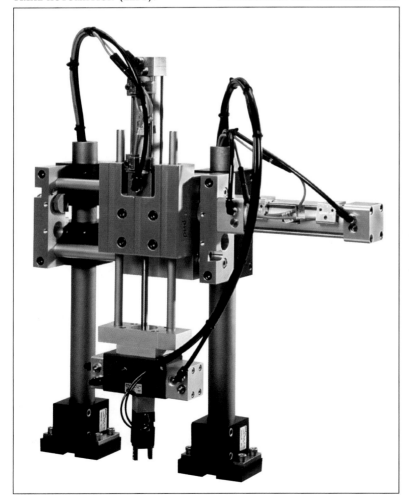

understand the need for quick turnaround. With a track record of more than 98 percent on-time shipments, employee dedication is quite evident. Many standard products ship within 48 hours, while most custom products are quoted quickly and accurately within two working days.

The company also delivers by providing engineering software that saves customers time when designing equipment and machinery. "We're establishing PHD as a company that's easy to do business with," states President and CEO Joe Oberlin, "and the software is just one way of doing that." The company's CD-ROM is updated quarterly with continually enhanced features to guide customers through equipment design and problem solving. PHD's Designer's Resource™ CD-ROM is the best of its kind in the industry due to its parametric CAD configurator software, product sizing software, CAD library, product and application videos, and complete digital catalog. This complete package of technical information saves design engineers hours of time and eliminates risk. As a result, PHD provides significant value to its customer, while proving itself the innovative leader in the industrial automation industry.

PEOPLE: THE MOST IMPORTANT ASSET

Since 1957, employees have worked in teams, a concept that has molded the company into a leading supplier of solutions and innovations. Along with the need to expand and improve its product lines, PHD also strongly supports employee development. "We continue to attract, train, and retain a very talented and experienced work force that prides itself on developing and producing quality products and services," says Jerry Hannah, vice president of human resources. PHD's continuous improvement strategy is supported by a variety of training and development opportunities and is specifically directed toward upgrading employees' skills in a variety of areas, such as engineering, manufacturing, systems, quality, and leadership.

LOOKING INTO THE FUTURE

"Some companies want to be all things to all people," Oberlin says. "Although we once thought that way, now we want to focus on specific products and make those products well." PHD has worked hard to learn about its customers and their needs. By improving customer intimacy and taking an active role in solving customers' problems, PHD's employees are constantly creating new and pro- gressive partnerships. Service has always been and will continue to be a driving force of PHD, especially as the company looks to the future and defines its role in the industry.

As PHD moves aggressively into the future, it will be establishing customer-focused niches in specific markets. By emphasizing the development of specialized products to meet unique needs, and practicing rapid product deployment, PHD is strategically positioning itself to gain an even greater market share. For PHD, its employees, and the Fort Wayne community, that means a bright and exciting future.

WOODBURN DIAMOND DIE, INC.

In 1957, WOODBURN DIAMOND DIE, INC. STARTED OUT AS a very small producer of diamond wire dies near Fort Wayne in Woodburn. After decades of constant growth and development, it is now the second-largest company in the industry, with branches across the United States and around the globe.

Woodburn Diamond Die produces diamond wire drawing dies used to make wire, offering natural, mono-crystalline, and polycrystalline diamond materials in various size range capabilities and tolerances. In addition, the company produces guides, wipes, and carbide dies; dies for tinning, bunching, strand-ing, and enameling; and elongation dies and sets. Woodburn Diamond Die also offers recutting and inventory management services.

Although some of the company's largest customers are located in Fort Wayne and throughout Indiana, the majority of its business is focused in other parts of the United States. Woodburn Diamond Die also exports to Europe, Asia, and South America.

STRATEGIC LOCATION IN WOODBURN

More than four decades ago, company founders Cleland Farver and Junior Knapp chose to establish their business in Woodburn because of its proximity to Fort Wayne. Often considered the diamond die capital of the world, Fort Wayne was also home to many of the company's original customers. In 1970, after Farver's retirement, his son, Rex Farver, took over his interest in the company. Around that same time, Woodburn Diamond Die began using lasers in the production process, establishing itself as one of the first in the industry to embrace this technology. The transition to lasers propelled Woodburn Diamond Die into a position as a world leader and the number two powerhouse in its industry.

In 1976, Rex Farver bought out Knapp's interest in the business, and today, Farver runs the company as president. Other Farver family members also serve as part of Woodburn's 70-person Indiana workforce.

GLOBAL EXPANSION

In addition to its original headquarters, Woodburn Diamond Die has facilities in Charlevoix, Michigan; Juarez, Mexico; and Surat, India; as well as a distributorship in Germany. In total, the company employs 200 workers around the globe.

Because many of its customers in the automotive industry have begun moving to Mexico in recent years, Woodburn Diamond Die established its Juarez facility in 1997 to service clients' needs. In India, the company has operated since 1997 as Walson Woodburn Wire Die Private Ltd., a joint venture with a wire die manufacturer already established in India. While the company's Mexican facility will serve customers in Central and South America, its plant in India will focus on markets primarily in Asia.

Woodburn Diamond Die opened its two foreign operations so it could maintain a strong presence in the global market. According to Farver, the biggest challenge the company has faced in the last decade has been increased world-wide competition. "More and more companies around the world are trying to come into the market," he says, adding that duties into foreign countries have also posed challenges for U.S. companies that export their products. "To maintain our position, we had to expand into other countries."

MANY OF WOODBURN DIAMOND DIE, INC.'S ORIGINAL CUSTOMERS WERE LOCATED IN FORT WAYNE, WHICH IS CONSIDERED BY MANY TO BE THE DIAMOND WIRE DIE CAPITAL OF THE WORLD. THE COMPANY MAINTAINS HEADQUARTERS IN NEARBY WOODBURN, INDIANA.

SERVICE AND QUALITY: TOP PRIORITIES

Since its founding, Woodburn Diamond Die has operated with a serious focus on service and quality. "We strive to do our best for our clients," Farver says. "Not only do we make first-class products, but we also offer service, putting our customers' needs first and working to establish a strong relationship with them."

As for its products, Woodburn Diamond Die offers among the highest precision and accuracy in the industry. According to Farver, this is due in large part to the heavy investment the company has made in high-precision, state-of-the-art equipment. Furthermore, such high quality is the result of teamwork: Woodburn Diamond Die considers its employees, many of whom have worked for the company almost 30 years, to be one big family.

Woodburn Diamond Die is one of the few companies to offer a full product line of dies, from the smallest imaginable sizes (sometimes thinner than a human hair) to the largest. It manufactures 600 types of dies and makes specialty products for its customers' unique needs.

Essentially, Woodburn Diamond Die's product line consists of natural diamond dies using anywhere from 5-point to 2-carat diamonds. It also produces man-made polycrystalline dies, which require 10-point to 50-carat diamonds. Although Woodburn Diamond Die does not sell directly to consumers, Farver estimates

that every day millions of people use products that have been drawn through its diamond dies.

COMMITTED TO THE COMMUNITY

Outside its global business, Woodburn Diamond Die plays a big part in its hometown community, sponsoring local baseball and softball teams. And every year, its employees fill the space underneath the company's Christmas tree with gifts for

children at the Woodburn Christian Children's Home.

Rex Farver is optimistic about the future of Woodburn Diamond Die. He sees its position in the world market strengthening as it captures more business overseas. No matter how much the company grows, though, there is one thing that will not change: the company's commitment to the customer. As Farver himself says, "We will always offer our customers service they can't find anywhere else."

THE HIGH PRECISION AND ACCURACY OF WOODBURN DIAMOND DIE'S PRODUCTS ARE DUE IN LARGE PART TO THE HEAVY INVESTMENT THE COMPANY HAS MADE IN HIGH-PRECISION, STATE-OF-THE-ART EQUIPMENT. SUCH HIGH QUALITY IS ALSO THE RESULT OF TEAMWORK: THE COMPANY CONSIDERS ITS EMPLOYEES TO BE ONE BIG FAMILY (TOP LEFT AND RIGHT).

WOODBURN DIAMOND DIE PRODUCES DIAMOND WIRE DRAWING DIES USED TO MAKE WIRE, OFFERING NATURAL, MONOCRYSTALLINE, AND POLYCRYSTALLINE DIAMOND MATERIALS IN VARIOUS SIZE RANGE CAPABILITIES AND TOLERANCES (BOTTOM).

WPTA-TV 21ALIVE

SINCE 1989, WPTA-TV 21ALIVE HAS BEEN THE number one station in Fort Wayne, making this ABC affiliate Northeast Indiana's news provider of choice. In fact, more area residents get their local news from 21Alive than any other news service, including radio stations, other television stations, and newspapers.

The station's market, or audience, consists of 12 counties: Adams, Allen, DeKalb, Huntington, Jay, Noble, Steuben, Wabash, Wells, and Whitley counties in Indiana, and Paulding and Van Wert counties in Ohio. During an average week, nearly 85 percent of the homes in this market tune in 21Alive at one time or another, and over a four-week period, 21Alive reaches 95 percent of the households in the market.

When 21Alive first went on the air in 1957, it faced tough competition. NBC and CBS had already established a presence in the area, and one of the earliest challenges was getting people to switch to 21Alive, which at the time was owned by Sarkes Tarzien. In the years that followed, the station gradually attracted more and more viewers.

In 1973, WPTA was sold to Combined Communications Corp., and a year later, General Manager Ed Metcalfe joined the station and established a tradition of serving the community. During his tenure, the station underwent yet another change in ownership, as Combined Communications merged with Gannett in 1979, and then was bought by Pulitzer in 1983. In 1989, the station was sold to Granite Broadcasting, which remains its owner today.

CONTINUING A TRADITION

After Metcalfe retired, Barbara Wigham stepped in as general manager and expanded the station's service to the community. Rather than simply reacting to community needs, the station began assessing those needs and implementing strategies to meet them.

Today, under President and General Manager Jerry L. Giesler, the station and its 100 employees continue the long-standing tradition of serving the community. Every year, the station plots a calendar of its community events, which are headed by Jan D'Italia. Some of the station's most prominent events include Focus on Health, Festival of Trees, the Jefferson Awards, and One of a Kind.

Giesler also credits the station's success to the talent of 21Alive's many broadcast journalists who know the area and have become trusted friends of the community. They include Keith Edwards, Jane Hersha, Victor Locke, Melissa Long, Dean Pantazi, and Jay Walker. Today, the station is growing its second generation of broadcast journalists, who will someday have the same strong ties with the community.

UNIQUE PROGRAMMING FEATURES

Talent is only one ingredient in 21Alive's success. Under the direction of News Director Don Bradley, the station's knack for reporting local news is the major

WPTA-TV 21ALIVE NEWS ANCHORS KEITH EDWARDS AND MELISSA LONG ARE TWO OF FORT WAYNE'S MOST RECOGNIZABLE PERSONALITIES.

A DAILY EDITORIAL MEETING WILL
DECIDE THE FOCUS OF THE EVENING
NEWS. UNDER THE DIRECTION OF
NEWS DIRECTOR DON BRADLEY,
THE STATION'S KNACK FOR REPORT-
ING LOCAL NEWS IS THE MAJOR
DIFFERENCE BETWEEN 21ALIVE
AND OTHER STATIONS.

difference between 21Alive
and other stations.

"We tell people what's hap-
pened in Fort Wayne today,"
Giesler says, "and if a national
story has local impact, then we'll
tell people what that local impact
is." The world news is featured in
a segment called the First Seven
Minutes of News, which airs
during the opening minutes of
the 11 p.m. newscast and gives
viewers a thumbnail sketch of
the day's national and international events.

From Monday through Friday,
21Alive produces 3.5 hours of
local news each day, airing news-
casts at 5:30 a.m., noon, and 5, 6,
and 11 p.m. The station offers a
unique variation to the usual head-
lines through its Good News
segment by digging up acts of
kindness in the community and
featuring them in Good News.
Because of this segment, 21Alive
has earned a reputation as the
Good News Station.

Eric Olson's 21 Country is
another important part of the
newscast. Olson finds unusual
stories that happen in the 12-
county viewing area and then
reports on them every Tuesday,
Wednesday, and Thursday at
6 p.m., and Sundays at 6 and 11
p.m. Also, Jennifer Blomquist

recognizes people once a week
for an anniversary or a birthday
in a segment called Sunshine
Spotlight.

THE EMOTIONAL SIDE
OF STORIES

Rather than simply talking about
hard facts and figures, 21Alive
reporters bring an emotional side
into their stories. Covering a plant
closing in Fort Wayne typically
involves talking with the mayor,
the chamber of commerce, and
plant owners. But for 21Alive
reporters, the story isn't only
about the impact on the local
economy; it also concerns the
25-year-old man who lost his
job and has to relocate his family
to another community—even

though his wife's mother and
grandmother live in Fort Wayne.
That's what Giesler calls the heart
of the story. "If we can get to the
heart of the story regularly," he
says, "then we're doing our job."

In the next decade, 21Alive
will invest millions of dollars to
convert its equipment to digital
technology. As the station makes
this transition, Giesler foresees
no differences in the emotional
connection 21Alive already makes
with its audience. "If we're responding to human needs and
connecting on an emotional level
with the audience, then the future
will look like the present," Giesler
says. "No matter how much technology advances, we'll still have
human needs that are timeless."

WPTA-TV HAS BEEN AN ABC
AFFILIATE IN FORT WAYNE
SINCE 1958.

INDIANA UNIVERSITY-PURDUE UNIVERSITY FORT WAYNE

A STATE-ASSISTED UNIVERSITY SERVING INDIANA'S SECOND-largest city and the surrounding region, Indiana University-Purdue University Fort Wayne is a combined campus of these two Big 10 schools. The university, known locally as IPFW, takes advantage of the best features and resources these institutions have to offer.

The university was officially dedicated in November 1964, but its roots were planted years ago through connections to branches of Indiana University (IU) and Purdue University. In 1917, classes began at the IU extension in Fort Wayne. A branch of Purdue University was opened in Fort Wayne in 1941. In the 1950s, talks began to combine the two schools, and the Indiana-Purdue Foundation was formed. In 1964, IPFW became an official entity and a pioneer of regional joint ventures between major state universities. This model would be copied in other Indiana communities and elsewhere around the country.

Today, IPFW ranks as the sixth-largest institution of higher education in Indiana, enrolling approximately 11,000 students in daytime, evening, and weekend classes year-round, and employing close to 1,100. Catering to the diverse educational needs of the area, IPFW serves students ranging in age from 13 to 79, with the average age being 26.

TOP REASONS TO ATTEND IPFW
Students choose IPFW for various reasons. Value plays a key role in their decision: IPFW offers an affordable education, with class fees among the lowest of Indiana's four-year universities. And approximately 50 percent of IPFW's students receive some form of financial aid.

IPFW also affords choices. More than 175 degree options are available, and since 1964, more than 41,000 degrees have been granted. Students can choose from associate, bachelor's, or master's degrees, and certificate programs, and can attend classes on either a full-time or a part-time basis. IPFW also offers continuing

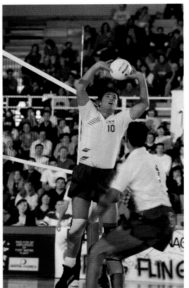

studies to nearly 10,000 participants who choose from 675 courses, seminars, and workshops. Additionally, contracted credit and noncredit programs are presented on-site to numerous businesses and industries.

Undoubtedly, atmosphere sets IPFW apart. Although the university is linked to two large universities, students receive the personal attention of a midsize campus. Nearly 80 percent of classes have fewer than 25 students. Those students receive the highest-quality education from professors and instructors who excel in their fields.

In addition, flexibility plays a role in a student's decision to attend IPFW. The university offers classes during the day or evening and on weekends, on or off campus, or via cable TV or the Internet.

A COMPLETE COMMUNITY FOR STUDENTS
Campus activities abound at IPFW, where more than 50 organizations help students make the most of their college experience. The Student Activities Office oversees the activities of the departmental clubs, honorary societies, religious organizations, Greek organizations, and special

INDIANA UNIVERSITY-PURDUE UNIVERSITY FORT WAYNE (IPFW) STUDENTS HAVE THE OPPORTUNITY TO PLAY A VARIETY OF COLLEGIATE SPORTS, INCLUDING BASEBALL, BASKETBALL, CROSS-COUNTRY, SOCCER, SOFTBALL, TENNIS, TRACK, AND VOLLEYBALL (TOP).

ALTHOUGH IPFW IS LINKED TO TWO LARGE UNIVERSITIES, STUDENTS RECEIVE THE PERSONAL ATTENTION OF A MIDSIZE CAMPUS. MOST CLASSES HAVE FEWER THAN 25 STUDENTS, WHO RECEIVE THE HIGHEST-QUALITY EDUCATION FROM PROFESSORS, INSTRUCTORS, AND COUNSELORS WHO EXCEL IN THEIR FIELDS (BOTTOM LEFT AND RIGHT).

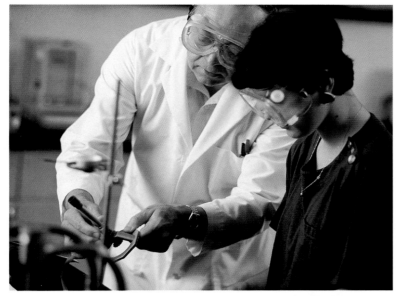

interest clubs. Students can join the staff of the *Communicator*, the student newspaper; participate in recreational and intramural sports; take part in student government; act in or manage plays put on by the Department of Theatre; explore college musical interests; or produce programs for Channel 56, a cable access channel run by IPFW.

Students also have the opportunity to play a variety of collegiate sports. IPFW competes in the NCAA at the Division II level, and is a member of the Great Lakes Valley Conference and the Midwest Intercollegiate Volleyball Association. Both men and women compete in basketball, volleyball, tennis, cross-country, and track; men compete in baseball and soccer, and women compete in softball and soccer.

COMMUNITY PARTNERSHIP

Through its many partnerships and community service ventures, IPFW has established itself as a major contributor to Fort Wayne's economic development, social welfare, and cultural life. The university considers itself an integral part of the community, just as the community is an integral part of the university.

For example, IPFW is partnering with the City of Fort Wayne and the Greater Fort Wayne Chamber of Commerce to establish the Northeast Indiana Innovation Center. The business park will combine medical, technological, and industrial components to help entrepreneurs get a success-

ful start. Plans are also under way to construct the university's first residence halls. In addition, IPFW's department of nursing has teamed with Parkview Hospital to provide nursing students with paid opportunities and to expand the job pool of available nurses for hire at the health care facility.

Community partnerships include those with Fort Wayne Community Schools. Through different programs, high school students are given opportunities to collaborate with IPFW faculty members on research and to explore collegiate options. IPFW is also working with Stop Child Abuse and Neglect (SCAN) to create a children's garden.

IPFW hosts the Omnibus Lecture Series, an annual, six-lecture series dedicated to the preservation of diverse ideas, the summer Performances on

the Plaza series, visiting lecturers, and Lunch with a Scientist at Science Central.

A FUTURE IN EXCELLENCE

Long-range plans for IPFW include continued improvement of undergraduate teaching, expansion of library collections and other forms of undergraduate research support, increased academic and fiscal autonomy, expansion of facilities to accommodate increased enrollment, attraction and retention of a more heterogeneous student body, and increased outside funding of faculty research.

Since its founding in 1964, IPFW has evolved into a thriving educational institution that offers a unique, high-quality education. The campus will continue to develop as it addresses the needs of its students and the surrounding region.

CLOCKWISE FROM TOP LEFT: IPFW OFFERS A WIDE VARIETY OF STUDIES; MORE THAN 175 DEGREE OPTIONS ARE AVAILABLE.

THE FRIENDS PAVILION IS A POPULAR PLACE FOR STUDENT ACTIVITIES ON CAMPUS. MORE THAN 50 ORGANIZATIONS HELP STUDENTS MAKE THE MOST OF THEIR COLLEGE EXPERIENCE.

IPFW HAS EVOLVED INTO A THRIVING INSTITUTION THAT OFFERS A UNIQUE, HIGH-QUALITY EDUCATION.

SINCE 1964, IPFW HAS GRANTED MORE THAN 41,000 DEGREES, INCLUDING ASSOCIATE, BACHELOR'S, OR MASTER'S DEGREES, AND CERTIFICATE PROGRAMS.

GENERAL CREDIT UNION

for the variety of financial services it offers, General Credit Union strives to be the primary financial institution for its members. "Our goal is to assist members in making business transactions that will help them grow and become more financially stable," says Jerry Yerkes, president.

In 1960, employees of General Telephone Company established the GTC Fort Wayne Federal Credit Union. Six years later, the credit union moved to the corner of Fourth and Harrison streets. In 1969, the credit union relocated to Clinton Street, and then to Memorial Way in 1978. The corporate headquarter's office at Mutual Drive opened in 1994.

The credit union adopted the name General Federal Credit Union in 1984. Fourteen years later, it became a state-chartered, privately insured credit union known as General Credit Union, and acquired Insurance Employees Federal Credit Union, doubling in assets and memberships.

CONVENIENCE THROUGH ACCESSIBILITY

Today, General Credit Union serves more than 14,000 members, all of whom belong to one of more than 100 employer groups. The credit union's 40 employees offer a full line of financial services at three locations in Fort Wayne.

General Credit Union strives to make its services more accessible to its members. They can make transactions at Credit Union Service Centers of Fort Wayne (CUSCFW), a joint effort between General Credit Union and two other local credit unions. The CUSCFW opened in 1996 as a branch office of the three credit unions. In addition, there are many other service centers around Indiana that General Credit Union members can use.

Shared branching provides yet another convenience to General Credit Union members. According to Kathy Knight, director of member services, General Credit Union is currently partnering with other credit union groups to offer services in more than 30 states, including Texas, Florida, and Georgia.

UNIQUE FINANCIAL SERVICES

General Credit Union houses two companies under its roof that work for the benefit of members. Member's Mortgage offers options in home financing, while Key Financial Group provides tax, payroll, and investment services.

General Credit Union also works to educate its members. The firm produces monthly newsletters, provides seminars, and sponsors a program—featuring Lucas the Lion—that helps children learn how to save money. Another club for all members over 55 provides discounted financial services and hosts various trips around the region.

Since its founding, the credit union has been an active member of the community. In the past, it has raised money for Riley Children's Hospital, Erin's House, and the American Cancer Society. The company also adopts families at Christmas, and donates money, clothing, and toys to them.

"We are in the business of people helping people," Yerkes says. "And that applies not only to our members, but to the entire community."

CLOCKWISE FROM TOP: "WE ARE IN THE BUSINESS OF PEOPLE HELPING PEOPLE," SAYS JERRY YERKES, PRESIDENT AND CEO OF GENERAL CREDIT UNION. "AND THAT APPLIES NOT ONLY TO OUR MEMBERS, BUT TO THE ENTIRE COMMUNITY."

GENERAL CREDIT UNION MEMBERS ENJOY A WIDE VARIETY OF LOW-COST FINANCIAL SERVICES.

A FULL-SERVICE BRANCH LOCATION, AS WELL AS EXECUTIVE OFFICES, IS LOCATED AT GENERAL CREDIT UNION'S CORPORATE HEADQUARTERS ON MUTUAL DRIVE IN FORT WAYNE.

FORT WAYNE
CITY *of* SPIRIT

© BUD LEE

HOLIDAY INN NORTHWEST/HOLIDOME

THE HOLIDAY INN NORTHWEST/HOLIDOME TREATS EVeryone like royalty; the hotel wants its guests to feel as if the red carpet has been rolled out. The goal is simple: to provide memorable experiences for all of its guests. Judging from the way the property is often fully booked, there's every indication the

Holiday Inn Northwest/Holidome is meeting that goal.

Established in Fort Wayne in 1968, the Holiday Inn Northwest/Holidome is a full-service hotel that caters to business and leisure travelers. Although it started as part of Holiday Inns, Inc., it is today a franchise independently owned by MB Inns, Inc. and operated by I.D.M., Inc.

FORT WAYNE'S LARGEST HOTEL

The Holiday Inn Northwest/Holidome—with 260 rooms, including three parlors, two hospitality suites, 114 kings, and 141 doubles—is Fort Wayne's largest hotel. As one of the city's finest, the hotel spent nearly $4 million to upgrade its facilities in 1997, modernizing the exterior appearance, renovating all of the guest rooms, and replacing an indoor miniature golf course with the new, two-story Adventure Play Area for children.

During the week, the Holiday Inn Northwest/Holidome caters primarily to a business clientele that enjoys the hotel's easy access to Interstate 69, close proximity to area companies, and numerous on-site amenities. One of the hotel's new features is a 28-room concierge level with a lounge that offers a complimentary breakfast as well as evening cocktails and hors d'oeuvres Monday through Thursday. Meeting facilities, including a boardroom on the con-

cierge level, another executive boardroom, and the Summit Ballroom, can accommodate anywhere from 10 to 300 people and offers the latest audiovisual equipment to meet guests' requirements. For business travelers who need to remain in Fort Wayne for a month or more, the Holiday Inn Northwest/Holidome offers extended-stay packages starting at 30 days.

On weekends, the hotel hosts groups as well as family and leisure travelers. Many of these guests stay at the Holiday Inn Northwest/Holidome to be close to the Fort Wayne Children's Zoo, Glenbrook Mall, sporting events at the Allen County War Memorial Coliseum and Expo Center, the Auburn Cord Duesenberg Museum, the Lincoln Museum,

CLOCKWISE FROM TOP:
THE HOLIDAY INN NORTHWEST/HOLIDOME'S BANQUET FACILITIES CAN ACCOMMODATE ANYWHERE FROM 10 TO 300 PEOPLE.

THE 26,000-SQUARE-FOOT HOLIDOME RECREATIONAL CENTER, THE LARGEST OF ITS KIND IN THE MIDWEST, HOUSES THE NEW, TWO-STORY ADVENTURE PLAY AREA, WHICH FEATURES A SPACE-SHIP AND A MAZE OF WORM SLIDES.

ESTABLISHED LOCALLY IN 1968, THE HOLIDAY INN NORTHWEST/HOLIDOME IS A FULL-SERVICE HOTEL THAT CATERS TO BUSINESS AND LEISURE TRAVELERS.

and Science Central. Because the hotel is located so close to the coliseum, it frequently counts musical entertainers, movie stars, and out-of-town sports teams among its overnight guests.

HOME OF THE HOLIDOME

In addition to its location near area attractions, the Holiday Inn Northwest/Holidome is home to its very own attraction. The 26,000-square-foot Holidome Recreational Center, the largest of its kind in the Midwest, features a heated indoor pool, a whirlpool and sauna, table tennis, billiards, a spaceship and worm slides in the new play area, and a gazebo. A fitness center with cardiovascular equipment and weights is also located in the Holidome for exclusive use by hotel guests. From Sundays through Thursdays, the Holidome can be rented for birthday parties and other events. On Friday and Saturday evenings, it features entertainment for the entire family, including magicians and caricature artists.

As part of the hotel's desire to provide every service to guests, the Holiday Inn Northwest/Holidome features Cassidy's Restaurant, which serves breakfast, lunch, and dinner. Cassidy's

Lounge also serves food and offers other forms of entertainment during regular business hours, such as a dartboard, shuffleboard, jukebox, dance floor, and billiard tables.

The Holiday Inn Northwest/Holidome offers banquet facilities that can seat 10 to 300 guests. Along with hosting wedding receptions and banquets, the hotel has welcomed a number of events for nonprofit organizations, such as the Taste of Fort Wayne, a fund-raiser for the American Heart Association in which attendees sample food from area restaurants.

Because the community uses the facility so often, the hotel feels it is only fair to return that support. In fact, the Holiday Inn Northwest/Holidome extends its community commitment to several high-profile events, acting as the sponsor hotel for the Standard Federal Balloon Classic, the Three Rivers Festival, and the Muddy River Run.

TEAM EFFORT

For the past several years, the Holiday Inn Northwest/Holidome has teamed with the Allen County Convention and Visitors Bureau to offer overnight packages tied

into the city's many attractions. Those popular packages, for example, might include several nights at the hotel and tickets to a Fort Wayne Wizards baseball game, a visit to one of the area's fine museums, or a trip to the Fort Wayne Children's Zoo.

As meetings and other large events have become increasingly important to the city's prosperity, the Holiday Inn Northwest/Holidome has worked closely with the bureau in bidding on various conventions. In fact, it is the host hotel for several conventions that are held annually in Fort Wayne. Overall, the Holiday Inn Northwest/Holidome hosts about 300 events each year, including conventions, wedding receptions, and family gatherings.

The hotel welcomes visitors who come to Fort Wayne not just for the attractions it offers as Indiana's second-largest city, but also for its hometown flavor. Guests looking for a memorable experience can rely on the Holiday Inn Northwest/Holidome, where big-city convenience and hometown hospitality make for a very pleasurable stay.

CLOCKWISE FROM LEFT: OFFERING THE LATEST AUDIOVISUAL EQUIPMENT, THE HOTEL'S MEETING FACILITIES INCLUDE A BOARDROOM ON THE CONCIERGE LEVEL, ANOTHER EXECUTIVE BOARDROOM, AND THE SUMMIT BALLROOM.

THE HOLIDAY INN NORTHWEST/HOLIDOME PROVIDES BIG-CITY CONVENIENCE AND HOMETOWN HOSPITALITY, WHICH MAKE FOR A VERY PLEASURABLE STAY.

IN 1997, THE HOTEL SPENT NEARLY $4 MILLION TO UPGRADE ITS FACILITIES, MODERNIZING THE EXTERIOR APPEARANCE AND RENOVATING ALL OF THE GUEST ROOMS.

IVY TECH STATE COLLEGE

O SUCCEED IN TODAY'S WORKPLACE, EMPLOYEES MUST be equipped with the right skills. That's why an increasing number of Indiana residents turn to Ivy Tech State College to get the training they need to advance their careers. ◆ A public, technical college, Ivy Tech opened the doors to its Fort Wayne

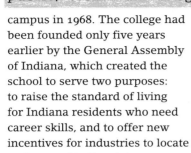

campus in 1968. The college had been founded only five years earlier by the General Assembly of Indiana, which created the school to serve two purposes: to raise the standard of living for Indiana residents who need career skills, and to offer new incentives for industries to locate and expand in the state.

Today, Ivy Tech in Fort Wayne is one of the college's 13 administrative regions and 24 major campuses located throughout Indiana. The Fort Wayne campus serves nine counties in Northeast Indiana from its North Anthony Boulevard location and through extension centers located throughout the region.

Ivy Tech offers more than 40 programs in four divisions: business, general education, health and human services, and technology. Students in these programs can earn one-year technical certificates or two-year associate of science or associate of applied science degrees.

In the past several years, Ivy Tech's enrollment in Fort Wayne has grown at a steady rate. Its current enrollment averages ap-

proximately 4,300 students per semester. Edward Reed, director of regional relations, attributes the growth to one simple reason: "More than anything, people are realizing that we can help them get and keep jobs."

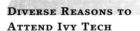

DIVERSE REASONS TO ATTEND IVY TECH

Students attend Ivy Tech for a number of reasons. According to Reed, the primary one is

to receive the education necessary to begin a new and more rewarding career in a short period of time.

Although many students pursue two-year degrees, there are just as many who need to take one or two courses to receive a promotion or add security to their jobs. To fill this need, Ivy Tech recently developed a career-oriented continuing education program. Currently, more than 1,000 students

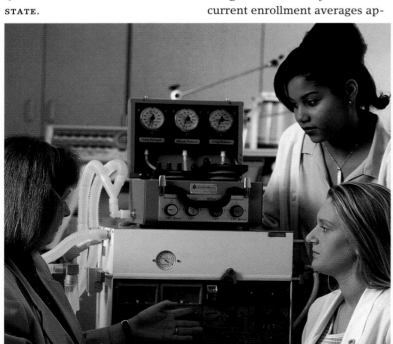

enroll in the college's continuing education classes each year.

Ivy Tech also works with community businesses to help them maintain a top-quality workforce. The college features a business and industry training division that can supply tailor-made programs to suit any business's needs. For example, a factory might require its employees to have a certain kind of training, whereas students would need a completely different set of skills to be productive in an office. Ivy Tech can design a training program for those employees around the skills they will need, and the college can then offer courses at its campus, the factory, or a neutral site.

COST, CONVENIENCE, AND QUALITY INSTRUCTION

In addition to receiving the training they need, students are attracted to other benefits at Ivy Tech. Perhaps the most important is cost; to make quality education available to more of the population, Ivy Tech offers the most affordable fees of any college in Indiana. Financial aid is also available.

In addition, students receive training from some of the most qualified instructors in the state. Ivy Tech currently employs more than 250 full- and part-time instructors. One of the institution's goals has been to keep the feel of small campus, and in fact, the average student-to-teacher ratio is 15-to-1. "Students aren't just a number here," Reed says. "We have worked hard to maintain a friendly, comfortable atmosphere."

Ivy Tech offers convenience in scheduling, an advantage for the many students who hold part- or full-time jobs or have

AMONG THE SCHOOL'S MANY ACADEMIC SPECIALTIES ARE ITS CULINARY ARTS PROGRAM (TOP) AND ITS STATE-OF-THE-ART HVAC LAB (CENTER).

CURRENTLY, MORE THAN 1,000 STUDENTS ENROLL IN CONTINUING EDUCATION CLASSES EACH YEAR AT IVY TECH (BOTTOM).

families. Day and evening classes are available, with almost 60 percent of the college's classes offered in the evening. Saturday classes are also becoming popular with the students. For the approximately 50 percent of Ivy Tech students who live outside Allen County, the college offers distance education courses via the Internet.

A GROWING CAMPUS

Continued growth will be a challenge into the future. Although Ivy Tech more than doubled the size of its campus in Fort Wayne since its founding—with expansions in 1976, 1981, and 1996—additional space will be needed

to accommodate the college's soaring student population. While the current location has no more room for growth, according to Reed, Ivy Tech is looking for land to expand its local campus.

Ivy Tech's growth mirrors the growth in the local business community, and Jon L. Rupright, vice president and chancellor of the Fort Wayne campus, sees this as an important component of Fort Wayne's economic development. "Because of the training we provide, employers can move into town knowing that they have a pool of trained employees to draw from," he says. "All of the benefits boil down to jobs. We're making individual lives better."

ALMET, INC.

The work of ALMET, INC. is an art that requires skilled craftsmanship and great attention to detail. Much of its work, though, goes unseen by the public eye, often being covered by brick, siding, and other building materials. ◆ Founded in 1969, Almet is a New Haven-based designer and fabricator of structural steel and miscellaneous metals, such as stairways and handrails, for the building industry. The name Almet stands for "all metals," and denotes the company's capability of producing various steel, aluminum, and stainless steel products. Although most of its clients are located primarily in the Midwest, the company has shipped products throughout the United States. It also manufactures a line of stationary and portable asphalt plants that are shipped to paving contractors worldwide.

EVOLUTION

Almet is the creation of four men who believed they could make a difference in the industry: Richard P. Greim, Robert H. Winkeljohn, Jackie D. Wickliffe, and Glen W. Schmidt. Almet's president, James R. Greim, is the son of cofounder Richard P. Greim.

The company started out by supplying miscellaneous metal fabrications for municipal wastewater treatment plants throughout the Midwest. As that market dwindled, Almet shifted its focus to fabricating structural steel. As the company gained experience with simple steel structures such as office buildings, schools, and retail stores, the miscellaneous metals became a minor part of the business.

Throughout the years, as Almet's expertise grew, so did the scope and complexity of its projects. In 1988, the company provided the structural steel framework for the Allen County War Memorial Coliseum expansion and the Exposition Center. In 1995, it completed the structure for the Purdue Bell Tower at Purdue University's main campus in West Lafayette. Other notable projects include the Lutheran and Dupont hospitals, the Norwest Bank Building, the Notre Dame natatorium, and the General Motors plant in Roanoke. In the mid-1980s, Almet began fabricating a line of asphalt producing equipment, a portion of its business known as ALmix. The ALmix product line includes cold feed bins, drum mixers, drag conveyors, bag-houses, and silos. The demand for ALmix equipment stems from its innovative design, which other manufacturers are starting to imitate. The company has patents pending on some of its machinery. ALmix plants have been shipped throughout the United States, as well as to Canada, Alaska, Russia, Africa, Korea, Australia, the Philippines, Malaysia, and Latin America.

In addition to building the ALmix asphalt equipment and supplying the company's general construction customers, Almet also provides custom fabrications for a wide variety of industrial customers.

CERTIFIED COMMITMENT

Several of Almet's strengths position it as a leader in its industry. The company was one of the first fabricators in Indiana to achieve the distinction of being an American Institute of Steel Construction (AISC)-certified shop. In addition, it was also one of the first 100 companies in the nation to achieve the AISC Category II certification, which states that

FOUNDED IN 1969, ALMET, INC. IS A DESIGNER AND FABRICATOR OF STRUCTURAL STEEL AND MISCELLANEOUS METALS SUCH AS HANDRAILS AND STAIRWAYS FOR THE BUILDING INDUSTRY. THE COMPANY'S HEADQUARTERS IS LOCATED IN ITS 100,000-SQUARE-FOOT OFFICE AND SHOP FABRICATION FACILITY.

Almet has the "personnel, organization, experience, procedures, knowledge, equipment, capability, and commitment to produce fabricated structural steel of the required quality" for conventional steel structures, simple steel bridges, and complex steel building structures. The company has also earned endorsements for sophisticated painting and fracture critical work.

Almet is one of the few fabricators to have a certified welding inspector and a professional engineer on staff. These strengths emphasize the company's attention to detail and its commitment to fabricating quality products. In addition to its AISC certification, Almet is a member of the Central Fabricators Association (CFA) and the Indiana Fabricators Association (IFA). These groups set the standards for the fabricating industry and are dedicated to promoting high-quality workmanship.

Almet's investment in two shot-blasting machines demonstrates its commitment to producing superior work. The shot-blasting process involves shooting chilled steel balls at the raw material to remove all scale and rust. The blasting process prepares the surface of the steel to allow for superior paint adhesion. Few other fabricators have this capability.

HONESTY, INTEGRITY, AND TEAMWORK

Almet's success is largely the result of its honesty, integrity, and teamwork. The company enjoys many excellent relationships with its customers in the building and asphalt industries. In fact, many of Almet's customers have main-tained long-term relationships since the company's creation and have come to rely on Almet to complete their projects. Since its beginning, Almet has never failed to complete a contract.

Teamwork is the guiding principle of the company's nearly 100 employees. The people at Almet are the company's most valuable asset, and everyone benefits from the success of the company through a profit-sharing program. The majority of Almet's employees have worked for the company more than 10 years.

THE FUTURE

For Almet, the future looks very exciting. The technology used today—both in production, like the shot-blasting and burning equipment, and in the products, such as the ALmix asphalt equipment—shows capabilities and a commitment to the industry that few other fabricators possess.

Almet is dedicated to continuing its leadership role in the fabricating industry. With business currently near capacity, the company has plans for substantial capital improvements to support existing and new customers for many years into the next century.

ALMET/ALMIX DESIGNS AND FABRICATES ASPHALT PLANTS, WHICH CONSIST OF COLD FEED BINS, BAGHOUSES, DRUM MIXERS, SILOS, DRAG CONVEYORS, AND CONTROL HOUSES.

IN 1995, ALMET FABRICATED AND SHIPPED THE STRUCTURE FOR THE 160-FOOT PURDUE BELL TOWER AT PURDUE UNIVERSITY'S MAIN CAMPUS IN WEST LAFAYETTE.

CANTERBURY GREEN

BUILT ON WHAT WERE ONCE JOHNNY APPLESEED'S stomping grounds, Canterbury Green today is a unique community spreading over 200 acres in Fort Wayne. Described as "the only way to live," the community has a lot to offer its residents. ◆ Canterbury Green broke ground in 1970, and during

BUILT ON WHAT WERE ONCE JOHNNY APPLESEED'S STOMPING GROUNDS, CANTERBURY GREEN TODAY IS A UNIQUE COMMUNITY SPREADING OVER 200 ACRES IN FORT WAYNE. DESCRIBED AS "THE ONLY WAY TO LIVE," THE COMMUNITY HAS A LOT TO OFFER ITS RESIDENTS.

the next nine years, went through eight phases of building. The result is a well-maintained community of more than 2,000 apartment units, including 115 executive suites.

ACTIVE LIFESTYLES

Canterbury Green offers a community within a community. It is situated with easy access to Glenbrook Square, Indiana University-Purdue University Fort Wayne, and the Allen County War Memorial Coliseum. The grounds include an 18-hole golf course and pro shop, jogging and walking trails, topiary gardens, soccer and softball fields, tennis courts, four swimming pools, clubhouse, fitness center, parks and picnic areas, stocked fishing ponds, billiards room, shuffleboard and sand volleyball courts,

racquetball and basketball courts, and an 18-hole miniature golf course.

Canterbury Green provides a lifestyle for all ages. A full-time activities director schedules daily activities geared for every age group. Events include bingo, aerobics, card groups, tennis lessons, craft making, billiard tournaments, theme dinners, poolside parties, and garden clubs.

To further meet the needs of residents, Canterbury Green has partnered with an in-home health care provider to offer home health assistance, aids, and medical equipment. Through Canterbury Green's Independent Living Program, residents can take advantage of meal services, nursing care, housekeeping, and an emergency response system.

CONVENIENT LIVING

Canterbury Green has the largest floor plans in Fort Wayne. Its one-, two-, and three-bedroom apartment homes and town homes feature 42 different floor plans, ranging from 728 to more than 1,800 square feet. Each unit is equipped with its own washer and dryer, and includes membership to the golf course and fitness center. "Our residents have all of the amenities of owning a home without having to worry about the maintenance of a home," says Thomas Deitche, property manager.

Recently, Canterbury Green instituted a Menu for Good Living program. When leases come up for renewal, residents can choose options to enhance their apartments and town homes. Those options include a wide range of

CANTERBURY GREEN'S ONE-, TWO-, AND THREE-BEDROOM APARTMENT HOMES AND TOWN HOMES FEATURE 42 DIFFERENT FLOOR PLANS, RANGING FROM 728 TO MORE THAN 1,800 SQUARE FEET.

free gifts such as sportswear, gift certificates to area restaurants, and U.S. Savings Bonds.

Canterbury Green is the only community in Fort Wayne that offers guaranteed maintenance. The maintenance team responds to all problems within 24 hours. "Our focus is customer service," Deitche says. "We want to make sure we're always meeting and exceeding the needs of our residents."

Surveys conducted by the management company continuously rank Canterbury Green as one of the top properties for fulfilling its residents' needs; it has placed first for the past five years. Canterbury Green also received an award from Indiana's state apartment association for best resident retention for three years in a row and landscaping for four years consecutively.

HOTEL ALTERNATIVE

Canterbury Green also provides an alternative to a hotel for people needing short-term accommodations, offering daily, weekly, and monthly rates whether for business or pleasure. Lodging at Canterbury Green features 115 executive suites, including the Presidential Suite measuring 2,200 square feet.

"Stay-and-play packages are offered to attract not only busi-

ness travelers, but also leisure travelers," says Chris Haintz, executive suite supervisor. Many people, even from as far away as Canada, for instance, spend summer vacations at Canterbury Green's suites to enjoy the golf and other amenities.

In addition, Canterbury Green has five rooms at the Roebuck Inn. Unlike the suites at Canterbury Green, the Roebuck Inn is a bed-and-breakfast built in 1849 and restored to provide antiquity as well as luxury. The house is often used for special occasions such as wedding parties, honeymoon packages, and weekend getaways. Its motto reads: "The only way to stay."

SUPPORTING THE COMMUNITY

Canterbury Green believes in giving back to the community. Since 1975, it has been a major donor to the Muscular Dystrophy Association (MDA). Years ago, when a resident's son contracted muscular dystrophy, the community raised money for his medical expenses. Those fund-raising efforts have since multiplied, and between 1975 and 1997, Canterbury Green raised more than $300,000.

Throughout the year, Canterbury Green sponsors various events like a haunted forest at Halloween and kids' carnivals. As a sponsor for the Three Rivers

Festival, Canterbury Green provides pontoon boat rides to raise money for MDA. Attracting the most attention, however, is the community's annual MDA Festival on Labor Day weekend. The highlight of the MDA Festival is an 18-hole golf tournament. "The response from residents as well as the public is so great that some golfers have to be turned away," says Andrea Hall, marketing director. Canterbury Green's community efforts also include donations of stay-and-play packages to various organizations.

Canterbury Green residents also look forward to the Groundhog Day Festival, an annual event since 1992. Every Groundhog Day, Canterbury Bill, the resident groundhog who has his own apartment, announces his predictions; his forecasts have even been featured on CNN. Festival events include a visit from the renowned General "Mad" Anthony Wayne on horseback, a Dixieland band, refreshments, and handouts like coffee mugs and balloons. Canterbury Bill also travels to dozens of schools to talk about the folklore of Groundhog Day.

If Bill were to predict the future for Canterbury Green, he would undoubtedly see a bright one. "We're not looking to get any bigger," Deitche says, "just better."

CONNOR CORPORATION

ONNOR CORPORATION WAS FOUNDED BY DR. CHARLES A. Wilson, and today, the plastic, hard rubber, and custom rubber molding supplier boasts more than 650 employees in facilities around the world, including 250 people in the Fort Wayne area, where Connor has its world headquarters. Connor's

LOCATED ON THE NORTHERN SIDE OF FORT WAYNE, CONNOR CORPO-RATION'S WORLD HEADQUARTERS IS CENTRAL TO DETROIT, CHICAGO, INDIANAPOLIS, AND CINCINNATI.

DRAWING FROM ALL WALKS OF LIFE, CONNOR IS LED BY A SEASONED, DIVERSE GROUP OF EXECUTIVES (BOTTOM RIGHT).

CEO DR. CHARLES A. WILSON (LEFT) AND PRESIDENT AND COO WILLIAM S. ESTHER BELIEVE CONNOR'S INVESTMENT IN PEOPLE, FACILITIES, MANUFACTURING EQUIP-MENT, STATE-OF-THE-ART COMPUT-ERS, AND THE LATEST SOFTWARE WILL HELP PROPEL THE GROWTH OF THE COMPANY (BOTTOM LEFT).

success has resulted from efforts that have been aptly described by the company's watchword: Creating solutions through a single source.

Since its founding, Connor Corporation has successfully provided cost-effective solutions in plastic, rubber, and related technologies for many industries, including automotive, HVAC, roofing, and medical. It is one of the top 50 plastic molders in the country, and the largest independent molder of battery containers and covers for the automotive market, supplying companies like Exide, East Penn, Delphi, and Trojan. With four divisions that specialize in specific molding capabilities, Connor Corporation also manufactures more cushion rings for fractional horse powered motors than any other company in the world.

GROWTH THROUGH ACQUISITIONS

The origins of the company go back to 1974, when two men founded a management consulting company called Corson Research; the name of the firm was derived from the last names of the founders, Edward Cornelia and Charles Wilson. In 1986, Wilson acquired Acro Custom Rubber, which was started in 1969 and is a manufacturer of

custom-molded rubber products with the capability of bonding rubber compounds to metal and plastic. Now known as the Rubber Products Division of Connor Corporation, its operations are located in a 47,000-square-foot facility in Fort Wayne. Its products include electric motor mounting rings, pump seals, bellows, torsion cords, gaskets, bumpers, grommets, and bushings.

In 1989, Wilson acquired a plastic molding operation called Jecto Custom Plastics, which has since been renamed as Connor's Engineered Plastics Division. A precision molder of engineered thermoplastic parts, this division

makes components for the recreational vehicle, environmental, computer, automotive, aircraft, electrical, electronic, appliance, and medical equipment industries. Its 25,000-square-foot facility is located in Fort Wayne.

Following this series of acquisitions, the manufacturing operations became known as the Corson Group. In 1995, the company expanded even further with the acquisition of the Richardson Battery Division of the Witco Corp. Started in the late 1800s, Richardson was the first manufacturer of battery components. Now known as the Battery Components Division of Connor Corpo-

STEVE VORDERMAN

IN ADDITION TO A HIGHLY SEASONED EXECUTIVE STAFF, CONNOR BOASTS STRONG LEADERSHIP FROM ITS YOUNGER ASSOCIATES.

ration, this company unit is the leading manufacturer of battery containers and other plastic components. It operates from more than 500,000 square feet of manufacturing space divided between plants in Indianapolis and Philadelphia, Mississippi, and has a 45,000-square-foot distribution, sales, and customer service center in Pico Rivera, California.

In 1995, the consolidation of the manufacturing organizations officially became known as Connor Corporation. The company has since established a 35,000-square-foot rubber molding operation in Monterrey, Mexico. This Mexican joint venture produces a line of hard rubber products that includes battery containers, covers, and other parts.

COMPETITIVE, WORLDWIDE SCOPE

Connor Corporation operates a total of more than 120 rubber molding presses and 110 plastic injection-molding machines, giving it capabilities that few other companies in this competitive industry have. Although most of its business comes from the United States, Connor is active in international markets, such as South America, Egypt, and Europe. "We've remained on top because

of our range of capabilities," says Wilson, who today serves as CEO. "Our prices are also competitive, and we are responsive."

To remain competitive, Connor Corporation consistently reviews its processes, employs a high caliber of professionals, and maintains control through rigorous quality checks. In 1995, all of Connor's locations were granted ISO 9000 and QS 9000 certifications by the International Organization for Standardization.

RESPONSIVENESS AS A GUIDING PRINCIPLE

Connor Corporation remains true to its long-held business philosophy, which dictates responsiveness to customers and employees. "We have the capabilities and the engineering expertise to solve problems and respond to needs," says Wilson, who was nominated for northern Indiana's Entrepreneur of the Year Award in manufacturing in 1997 and was named Small Businessman of the Month by the city of Fort Wayne in 1985. "Because we're a people-oriented company, we're responsive to our customers and our employees." To continue responding to customers' needs by providing high-quality, cost-effective solutions, Connor in-

vested $5 million in 1996-1997 to update its plastics operations in Fort Wayne with state-of-the-art equipment.

Although Connor Corporation has faced some tough obstacles—including international competition—over the years, the company has managed to achieve success in Fort Wayne, a community in which Wilson feels comfortable doing business. When he reflects on how far the company has come, he says he is most proud of the reputation the company has made for itself since becoming known as Connor Corporation. "Everything leading up to that point took us to a level that few have been able to achieve," he says. "It's just amazing how we would stop the operations of major corporations if our parts weren't on time or if we didn't have the right quality. Today, we're a company that has to be reckoned with."

Connor feels its investment in people, facilities, manufacturing equipment, state-of-the-art computers, and the latest software will help propel the growth of the company. Looking to the future, Wilson expects the company to double in size within a five-year period, further solidifying Connor Corporation's position for decades to come.

CITY OF SPIRIT   231

MIDWEST TOOL & DIE CORPORATION

QUALITY AND SERVICE ARE THE BACKBONE OF MIDWEST Tool & Die Corporation, a small but successful Fort Wayne-based company that has managed to attract the attention of giants in the automotive and electronic industries. ◆ Midwest Tool & Die offers design, manufacturing, and stamping services.

It designs, builds, and runs progressive high-speed dies all within one facility—primarily for major customers in the automotive and electronic industries in the United States. According to President Victor Felger, the domestic market accounts for 70 percent of the company's business—the rest are overseas customers.

TREMENDOUS GROWTH

Midwest Tool & Die was the vision of three men who, in 1974, set out to create a world-class company that offered a three-part system of product and tool development. Those individuals were Felger; his father, Paul; and David Venderley, vice president of Mid-

west Tool & Die.

The company originally designed and built progressive high-speed dies. Eventually, more and more customers began to ask for small test runs of the dies, and in 1985, Midwest Tool & Die officially began to run dies for its customers.

Since 1991, the company has experienced such tremendous growth that it's gone through at least seven different expansions. Today, Midwest Tool & Die's facility spreads across 40,000 square feet.

SUCCESS THROUGH SERVICE AND QUALITY

Felger says two main attributes account for Midwest Tool & Die's growth: service and quality. "When

we design a die," he says, "we build service into that tool." Most of the dies Midwest Tool & Die builds run at 1,000 to 1,500 strokes per minute. If that tool were to break down, the customer would experience unnecessary downtime and product delays. That's why products from Midwest Tool & Die can be serviced while they're still in the press.

Quality is also a hallmark of Midwest Tool & Die. To ensure the highest quality, the firm performs audits on every product throughout the process. The company has invested millions of dollars in top-of-the-line, computer-driven technology that allows for minute, precise inspections of each and every tool. In addition, the temperature in the company's facility is controlled; the wire EDM area, for example, maintains a constant room temperature with no more than a one degree variance to produce accurate parts and hold tight tolerances.

To further guarantee the quality of the product, Midwest Tool & Die tests dies in one of its high-speed presses to locate any weak areas and to make engineering corrections. Customers often request that the company run one to 5 million parts just to

TO PRODUCE ACCURATE PARTS AND HOLD TIGHT TOLERANCES, MIDWEST TOOL & DIE CORPORATION'S WIRE EDM ROOM MAINTAINS A CONSTANT ROOM TEMPERATURE WITH NO MORE THAN A ONE-DEGREE VARIANCE (TOP).

MIDWEST TOOL & DIE DESIGNS, BUILDS, AND RUNS PROGRESSIVE HIGH-SPEED DIES ALL WITHIN ONE FACILITY IN FORT WAYNE (BOTTOM).

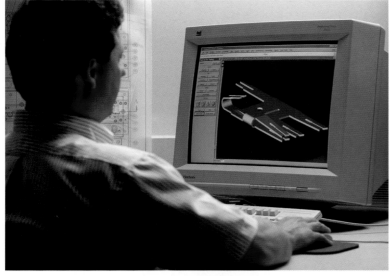

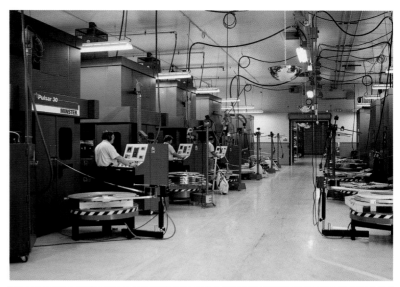

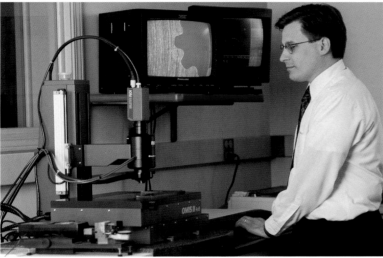

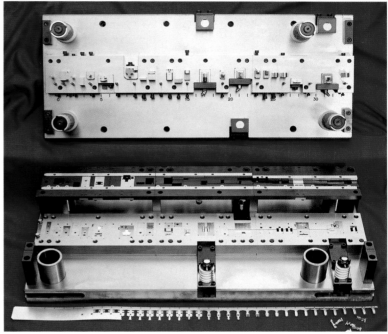

prove the tool.

At the request of its customers, Midwest Tool & Die will also send a toolmaker to their facilities to assist in the tool setup. The toolmaker will then show customers how to get the most benefit from the die and how to service that die.

The company's commitment to quality has been well recognized in the industry. In January 1998, Midwest Tool & Die achieved ISO/QS-9000 certification. In 1998 and 1999, it received the State of Indiana Quality Improvement Award.

TRAINING AND HIGH-TECH EQUIPMENT

Because Midwest Tool & Die produces such unique tools, built to run at extremely high speeds, its workforce consists of highly trained toolmakers. In fact, when the company hires a seasoned tool and die maker from the outside workforce, that individual must go through intensive training to understand the quality of

work the company demands.

Midwest Tool & Die also enlists three to four employees a year in its four-year apprenticeship program, which is accredited by the National Tool and Die Association. Graduates from the program must complete 648 hours of trade school training and 8,000 hours of on-the-job training. In addition, the company provides other training as needed for its employees. As Felger says, "Training is really the key to success."

The company has also invested heavily in state-of-the-art equipment to produce some of the industry's highest-quality products. Midwest Tool & Die continually updates its equipment to keep up with technology, something that has helped the company become such a success. "We're using technology to our advantage so that we can maintain quality," Felger says. "It's a challenge to keep up with the ever changing world of technology."

Computers, for example, help control many of the operations at Midwest Tool & Die. The engineers work with the latest computer-aided design technology, while the entire company is networked through computers to increase productivity.

GETTING BETTER, NOT BIGGER

Felger admits he never thought the company would grow to what it is today: "It's always fascinated me that as a small company in the middle of Indiana, we've had the ability in such a short period of time to supply tooling needs around the world."

Now that Midwest Tool & Die has grown to such a size, Felger wants to maintain the company's focus on quality and service. "I don't particularly care to get bigger," he says. "I just care to get better."

MIDWEST TOOL & DIE HAS INVESTED HEAVILY IN STATE-OF-THE-ART EQUIPMENT—INCLUDING SIX COMPUTER-AIDED DESIGN STATIONS (TOP LEFT), A TOP-QUALITY STAMPING AREA (TOP RIGHT), AND SEVERAL HIGH-TECH INSPECTION STATIONS (BOTTOM LEFT)—TO PRODUCE SOME OF THE INDUSTRY'S HIGHEST-QUALITY PRODUCTS, SUCH AS THE COMPLEX, HIGH-SPEED DIES (BOTTOM RIGHT).

FROM ITS BEGINNINGS AS A SMALL RECORDING STUDIO IN the home of Chuck Surack, Sweetwater has since grown to become one of the nation's leading retailers of professional audio equipment for studio and stage. ◆ Surack founded Sweetwater in 1979. Initially, the company provided recording

services to local and regional artists and businesses. Two things lead to the company becoming a music retailer. The first was Surack's frustration with trying to find a dependable, knowledgeable music equipment dealer. There didn't seem to be a dealer who could get Surack the equipment he needed, when he needed it. Prices could be outrageous, and the reliable technical service and support sometimes necessary with such specialized gear was almost impossible to find. Surack saw there was a definite need in the industry for that kind of comprehensive sales and support.

The second incentive was the introduction of the revolutionary Kurzweil K250 keyboard in the early 1980s. The K250 gave musicians access to all the instruments in an orchestra, opening up new avenues of composition and performance. Surack began creating his own sound and sample library for his K250. He soon became recognized in the music industry as an expert on this instrument.

SWEETWATER'S MAIN STUDIO, STUDIO A, FEATURES 48-TRACK DIGITAL RECORDING, A 200-INPUT EUPHONIX CONSOLE, AND A SEVEN-FOOT YAMAHA GRAND PIANO WITH MIDI.

Top musicians, including Stevie Wonder, Kenny Rogers, and many other professionals, began ordering Chuck's sounds for their K250s, and asking for his help in ordering factory options and accessories. Sweetwater became a Kurzweil dealer to fulfill these requests, and Surack began selling and servicing these products to help

his professional musician friends.

As the industry became more sophisticated, these friends/customers returned again and again to ask for more product advice. Surack acquired additional product lines, and the company's emphasis began to shift from recording studio to musical instrument retailer. Since then, Sweetwater has become one of the most successful and fastest-growing music retailers in the country, with more than 190 employees and a 40,000-square-foot facility that includes retail, studio, and communications departments. The company has been on *Inc.* magazine's list of the 500 fastest growing private companies three years in a row and has received the *Music Inc.* magazine REX Award for excellence in retailing.

Sweetwater works with a diverse group of clients from all over the world. Customers include high-profile professionals, musical hobbyists, amateur musicians, and multimedia companies that require audio equipment for everything from film soundtracks to video games. The company has installed MIDI and recording labs at many colleges—including Indiana University, which has the

SWEETWATER WORKS WITH A DIVERSE GROUP OF CLIENTS FROM ALL OVER THE WORLD. CUSTOMERS INCLUDE HIGH-PROFILE PROFESSIONALS, MUSICAL HOBBYISTS, AMATEUR MUSICIANS, AND MULTIMEDIA COMPANIES THAT REQUIRE AUDIO EQUIPMENT FOR EVERYTHING FROM FILM SOUNDTRACKS TO VIDEO GAMES.

largest installation of professional music workstations in academia.

ADDITIONAL DEPARTMENTS

The recording studio that started it all has grown with the rest of the company and remains an integral part of Sweetwater. Sweetwater Productions is a state-of-the-art recording facility consisting of three studio rooms running both tape and hard-disk recording systems. The main studio, Studio A, features 48-track digital recording, a 200-input Euphonix console, and a seven-foot Yamaha grand piano with MIDI.

Another department at Sweetwater is the Communications Group, a professional design and installation team for sound and video facilities. Established in 1997, the Communications Group offers consultation, design, and installation of communications and sound systems for businesses, hospitals, schools, churches, auditoriums, and many other forums. In 1998, the Sweetwater Communications Group completed a major renovation project for the Fort Wayne Embassy Theater, installing the first permanent sound system in the 2,500-seat theater built in the 1920s. Other projects include sound system design and renovation for the Foellinger Theater, the Cathedral of the Immaculate Conception, and the rebuilt St. Mary's Catholic Church.

REDEFINING CUSTOMER SERVICE

Sweetwater's success can be attributed to its customer-oriented approach to every aspect of the business. The company takes great pains to recruit the top people in the industry. Many employees have experience in professional sound and recording before coming to Sweetwater. New sales engineers receive extensive training and testing on music equipment knowledge, and attend classes in different aspects of music technology and sales almost daily. Sweetwater's world-class service and shipping departments both emphasize stellar customer service. Employees earn some of the highest salaries and use the most innovative and high-tech tools in the industry. The company's entire focus is on taking care of the customer. All training, whether technical or personal, in every department, is directed toward meeting this goal.

Marketing innovations include one of the first music-related Web sites, which went on-line at www.sweetwater.com in May of 1995. The site, one of the industry's largest, contains more than 4,000 pages and receives more than 3 million hits per month. In 1997, Sweetwater started *inSync*, the industry's first electronic daily newsletter, and in 1998, the company released its first equipment directory. All of Sweetwater's marketing and advertising is done in-house, including the design, maintenance, and hosting of the Web site, and the publication of the equipment directories and *Sweetnotes*, a bimonthly newsletter sent to more than 150,000 customers.

Sweetwater is also committed to the community. The company has been a long-time sponsor of the Fort Wayne Philharmonic and has underwritten its Young Artist Competition and many concerts. Sweetwater also supports the community's children by sponsoring the Foundation for the Arts and Music in Elementary Education (FAME) Festival and by providing music labs for area schools. In addition, the company sponsors a jazz stage at Fort Wayne's Three Rivers Festival, at which many employees donate their time and talents.

Surack has big plans for Sweetwater's future. By 2001, he anticipates sales in excess of $75 million. It's a challenge Sweetwater is looking forward to taking on. As Surack says, "We have an advantage in the retail music industry because we have the infrastructure, the support, and the people to make this company the best it can be."

CLOCKWISE FROM TOP LEFT: THE SWEETWATER HEADQUARTERS IN FORT WAYNE IS QUITE DIFFERENT FROM A TYPICAL MUSIC EQUIPMENT STORE.

SWEETWATER TAKES GREAT PAINS TO RECRUIT THE TOP PEOPLE IN THE INDUSTRY. NEW SALES ENGINEERS RECEIVE EXTENSIVE TRAINING AND TESTING ON MUSIC EQUIPMENT KNOWLEDGE, AND ATTEND CLASSES IN DIFFERENT ASPECTS OF MUSIC TECHNOLOGY AND SALES ALMOST DAILY.

ESTABLISHED IN 1997, THE SWEETWATER COMMUNICATIONS GROUP OFFERS CONSULTATION, DESIGN, AND INSTALLATION OF COMMUNICATIONS AND SOUND SYSTEMS FOR BUSINESSES, HOSPITALS, SCHOOLS, CHURCHES, AUDITORIUMS, AND MANY OTHER FORUMS.

SWEETWATER HAS INSTALLED MIDI AND RECORDING LABS AT MANY COLLEGES—INCLUDING INDIANA UNIVERSITY, WHICH HAS THE LARGEST INSTALLATION OF PROFESSIONAL MUSIC WORKSTATIONS IN ACADEMIA, WITH MORE THAN 80 KURZWEIL WORKSTATIONS CONNECTED TO MACINTOSHES AND PCS, RUNNING SEQUENCING AND NOTATION SOFTWARE.

REDiMED

WHEN THE FIRST REDiMED OPENED IN 1984, ITS managers wanted to change conventional thinking about who was in charge and who decided when patients would be seen. The new boss? The patient. This approach paid off. In the years since its creation, REDiMED has become one of

MEDICAL DIRECTOR DR. DEAN ELZEY, SENIOR VICE PRESIDENT LESLIE FENNIG, R.N., AND PRESIDENT DALE D. COCHARD DISCUSS EXPANDING REDiMED TO PROVIDE SERVICE TO OTHER COMMUNITIES IN INDIANA (RIGHT).

DALE D. COCHARD—PRESIDENT AND CEO OF REDiMED, AND ONE OF ITS ORIGINAL FOUNDERS—PRESENTS A LAYOUT FOR AN UPCOMING FACILITY. REDiMED HAS THREE OFFICES IN FORT WAYNE, AS WELL AS BRANCHES IN AUBURN AND HUNTINGTON (LEFT).

the area's top choices in medical care.

REDiMED's five clinics employ 150 and provide urgent care and occupational or industrial medicine 12 hours a day, 365 days a year. Urgent care makes up about 60 percent of the company's business, occupational medicine the other 40 percent.

REDiMED was the vision of four men, all of whom worked at Parkview Hospital: Dale D. Cochard, director of the emergency department at Parkview; Dr. Dean Elzey; Dr. Paul Blusys; and Dr. Albert Emilian. Today, Cochard is CEO of REDiMED, while Elzey serves as its medical director. When Lutheran Hospital of Indiana acquired REDiMED

in 1992, Blusys and Emilian left the staff. In 1995, REDiMED became part of a larger family when Quorum Health Group purchased Lutheran Hospital.

IMMEDIATE SUCCESS IN URGENT CARE

The original owners opened Fort Wayne's first REDiMED on Maplecrest Road. After witnessing the tremendous success of that center, they opened the second facility on Jefferson Boulevard in 1985. A third REDiMED soon followed on Cook Road. Eventually, REDiMED expanded to other communities. In 1998, it opened a center in Auburn as a joint venture with DeKalb Memorial Hospital. One year later, it introduced a facility in Huntington.

Still, there are dozens of other communities in need of a REDiMED. In fact, REDiMED has received requests from almost every county in the region to establish a facility in that particular area. Unfortunately, Cochard says, some communities don't have the population base to support a REDiMED.

A sizeable population is one reason REDiMED thrives in Fort

Wayne. When Cochard talks to people in the community, most of them have visited a REDiMED at least once. In fact, since the first REDiMED opened, the centers have treated more than 1 million visitors. That number continues to grow as more people become accustomed to the way REDiMED treats them when they walk through the door. Cochard calls it the culture behind REDiMED's success.

QUALITY CARE, QUALITY TREATMENT

REDiMED's customer service philosophy requires that patients be treated when they need medical attention—and at a location that's convenient for them—rather than waiting days or even weeks to see a doctor. The staff members try not to let the phones ring more than three times, and they greet every patient with a smile. Patients are seen quickly, and are treated in the order in which they arrive at the center unless a medical emergency takes precedence. This efficient service, Cochard notes, does not result in a loss of quality.

Having added occupational medicine to its services in 1988,

REDiMED considers itself a specialist in the field. Companies of all sizes utilize the occupational services to decrease time lost due to injury, and to create healthy work environments that reduce the number of on-the-job injuries. REDiMED provides a range of services that few others offer, including drug screens for area employers, medical care for on-the-job injuries, preemployment physicals, ergonomic issues in the workplace, and rehabilitation programs for employees who are injured.

CARING FOR THE COMMUNITY

REDiMED doesn't provide services just inside the walls of its facilities; it also gives to the community. Since its founding, the company has sponsored numerous children's sports teams, donating money to buy uniforms and equipment. It contributes to a variety of local nonprofit organizations such as the Fort Wayne Women's Bureau, the YWCA, and the Community

Harvest Food Bank. REDiMED also offers flu shots at most Scott's Food Stores during a two-week period every October.

In these changing times, health care facilities are faced with some of their biggest obstacles. REDiMED is prepared to meet the challenge. "We created this culture to meet our patients' needs," says Cochard. "Although it's becoming more difficult, we hope people understand that we try hard to be efficient, courteous, and convenient."

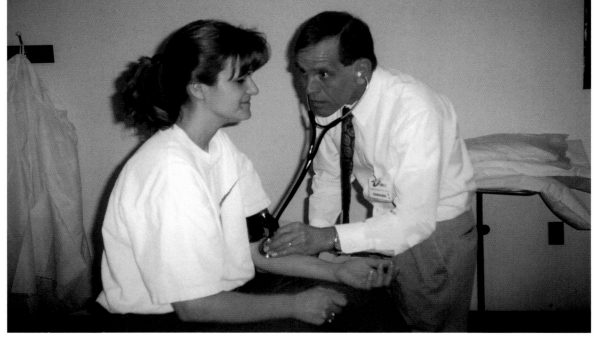

REDiMED's customer service philosophy requires that patients be treated when they need medical attention, rather than waiting days or even weeks to see a doctor. Samuel Shorter, PA-C, is one of many highly trained physician assistants who provide care to REDiMED's patients.

PEG PEREGO, U.S.A., INC.

FOR THE PAST 50 YEARS, PEG PEREGO HAS BEEN SPINNING its wheels for kids. Today, those wheels are still turning strong for the international company, which has made itself a household name in carriages, strollers, and children's riding vehicles. ◆ Peg Perego's story begins in a small town north of Milan, Italy, with a man named Giuseppi Perego, who made a baby carriage for his son Lucio. That single carriage marked the birth of an empire that began operations in Perego's modest garage. Originally, the company made only carriages, strollers, and juvenile products for children, but soon realized that the bulk of its sales occurred in the spring. Annual sales increased when Peg Perego added push-pedal, ride-on vehicles to its line for children. Those products were later modified to include battery-operated versions.

In 1964, Peg Perego opened its first overseas operation in Toronto, Ontario; four years later, the company built an assembly plant in Fort Wayne. Although the Indiana facility was sold in late 1984, Lucio Perego oversaw the opening two years later of a new Fort Wayne subsidiary called Peg Perego, U.S.A. Operations.

SUCCESS IN FORT WAYNE

Today, with 160 employees in Fort Wayne, Peg Perego, U.S.A. is responsible for the assembly, packaging, marketing, sales, and distribution of the company's juvenile and toy lines throughout the United States and Mexico. Juvenile products include carriages, strollers, and high chairs, and the toy lines include battery-powered and pedal-driven vehicles for children. While the majority of Peg Perego's worldwide manufacturing is based in Italy, the Fort Wayne branch has recently become involved in manufacturing most of the parts for the toys it assembles.

As Peg Perego has learned, Fort Wayne is an ideal location for its American operations. The city is strategically located to allow Peg Perego, U.S.A. to expand its distribution across the country. The cost of operating a business is also lower in Fort Wayne than in many other cities, providing opportunities for further growth and expansion. Because of its tremendous sales volume, Peg Perego, U.S.A. has undergone four major expansions. In 1987, the company moved into a 40,000-square-foot building. The following year, it added 60,000 square feet to that same building, which it currently occupies. Peg Perego, U.S.A. built another 60,000-square-foot facility in 1991 and recently completed a third building that adds another 125,000 square feet to the company's overall Fort Wayne presence.

DESIGN AND INNOVATION

A cosponsor of the Three Rivers Festival and a frequent contributor to dozens of community and charity organizations, Peg Perego, U.S.A. sells its toys directly to such retail giants as Toys "R" Us, Sears, and Kmart. Its juvenile line is sold through two specialty chains, Babies "R" Us and Baby Depot, as well as through juvenile specialty stores that have personnel to demonstrate unique features and advantages to customers—and to explain why Peg Perego products command a higher price than competitors'.

Design excellence and ongoing innovation are two specific reasons the company believes its

PEG PEREGO, U.S.A., INC. EXPANDED ITS ORIGINAL PRODUCT LINE TO INCLUDE PUSH-PEDAL, RIDE-ON VEHICLES LIKE THE GAUCHO GRANDE. SOME OF THOSE PRODUCTS WERE LATER MODIFIED TO INCLUDE BATTERY-OPERATED VERSIONS.

products rise above the competition. All Peg Perego products are designed the way Giuseppi Perego created his first carriage—with the child's safety in mind. Therefore, every product is durable, solid, and safe. The company is equally innovative when it comes to features. "We're generally the innovator when a new feature is developed for a stroller, high chair, or carriage," says Dale Schipper, vice president and general manager of Peg Perego, U.S.A. "Our challenge is to continue being innovative so we can maintain our place in the market."

Peg Perego has also become known for its selection of fabrics. With its world headquarters located near Milan—considered by many to be the fashion capital of the world—the company offers unique fabrics that are updated every year. "Fashion is an important word to us," says Ken Maxwell, director of marketing for Peg

Perego, U.S.A. "Beyond the appearance and function of our products is the fashion aspect."

Yet what works in Italy, where the designs originate, does not always work in the United States or in Canada, where Peg Perego has a sister company called Peg Perego Canada. "The basic concept is the same, but how you finish the product makes a difference in how appealing it is to the marketplace," Schipper says. Throughout the years, the company has worked to understand the different markets it serves and now feels confident it knows what each segment requires.

Quality Versus Quantity

All of Peg Perego's unique features result in high-quality products, and that is not about to change, according to Schipper. Even though more than 4 million babies are born every year in the United States, Peg Perego, U.S.A. sells

only 100,000 strollers each year. "We're not interested in quantity but rather quality," Schipper explains. "We want to do what we do better, which is why almost every time we go to Italy or they come to Fort Wayne, we spend most of our time discussing improvements and design changes that will make products more attractive, safer, or higher quality."

These words echo the thoughts of Giuseppi Perego on making his first carriage a half century ago. Says his son Lucio, who is considered Peg Perego's first customer, "We are only as good as the product we make." He adds that a majority of employees have been with Peg Perego for more than 20 years and, therefore, take tremendous pride in their work and the company's success: "We believe in our product, and we'll continue making it better for kids and parents."

A HOUSEHOLD NAME IN CARRIAGES, STROLLERS, AND CHILDREN'S RIDING VEHICLES, PEG PEREGO BELIEVES IN QUALITY OVER QUANTITY; THE COMPANY IS CONCERNED WITH SAFETY, INNOVATION, AND FASHION (RIGHT).

PEG PEREGO DESIGNS AND BUILDS PRODUCTS THE WAY FOUNDER GIUSEPPI PEREGO CREATED HIS FIRST CARRIAGE—WITH THE CHILD'S SAFETY IN MIND. THEREFORE, EVERY PRODUCT IS DURABLE, SOLID, AND SAFE (LEFT).

At MEDICAL IMAGING, PATIENTS DISCOVER A CARING staff and a friendly environment, two of the principles on which this radiology center was founded. ◆ A joint venture between Lutheran Hospital and a group originally known as C.F.B. Radiology (now Summit Radiology, P.C.), Medical

Imaging opened in 1987 as one of the first tenants of Lutheran Medical Park. Since then, it has grown tremendously, recently moving its billing and administrative services to a different floor in the medical building so it could expand its patient reception area and its examination and testing rooms.

FORT WAYNE'S LARGEST GROUP OF RADIOLOGISTS — SUMMIT RADIOLOGY, P.C.

Medical Imaging offers a complete range of diagnostic testing, including magnetic resonance imaging and angiography, more commonly known as MRI and MRA; spiral computed tomography, called CT or CAT scanning; ultrasound imaging; diagnostic X-ray; and mammography. Although most of its patients are referred to Medical Imaging by their doctors, women need no referral for mammography screenings.

The largest group of radiologists in Fort Wayne, Summit Radiology came about as a result of the merging of two groups,

C.F.B Radiology and Allen County Radiology. With more than 20 radiologists, Summit provides services for the patients of Medical Imaging, as well as Lutheran Hospital patients who come from some 23 counties in Indiana, Ohio, and Michigan. Summit radiologists also work with the patients of specialists in nearby cities like Chicago. In a day's time, it is not unusual for Medical Imaging to perform more than 100 imaging procedures.

STATE-OF-THE-ART EQUIPMENT

Since its founding, Medical Imaging has provided care using state-of-the-art equipment. Its radiologists, for instance, work and perform leading-edge studies with a high-field MRI unit, which is continuously being upgraded to incorporate the latest technology. In addition, Medical Imaging's mammography equipment features a variable tilt design that aligns with a woman's natural shape. The feature allows for maximum comfort and a clearer, more detailed view of a

larger area of breast tissue, thus providing a more accurate diagnosis. Medical Imaging is an FDA-certified, ACR-accredited mammography facility. It is also ACR-accredited in MRI and Ultrasound.

Medical Imaging's strengths also include same-day or next-day service. Because many of its patients see caregivers in other parts of Lutheran Medical Park, Medical Imaging coordinates testing and appointments with Lutheran Hospital and patients' doctors. It provides flexible scheduling, offering evening and Saturday appointments.

Medical lmaging also provides rapid results, with a turnaround time of 24 hours or less. An on-site radiologist is readily available to answer patients' questions, or to facilitate a quicker course of action if something unusual is spotted during a mammogram screening. All of this adds up to better care for the patients of Medical Imaging.

CARE AND COMPASSION
As the staff at Medical Imaging works to facilitate change in the

MEDICAL IMAGING OFFERS A COMPLETE RANGE OF DIAGNOSTIC TESTING, INCLUDING MAGNETIC RESONANCE IMAGING AND ANGIOGRAPHY, MORE COMMONLY KNOWN AS MRI AND MRA; SPIRAL COMPUTED TOMOGRAPHY, CALLED CT OR CAT SCANNING; ULTRASOUND IMAGING; DIAGNOSTIC X-RAY; AND MAMMOGRAPHY.

CLOCKWISE FROM TOP: A JOINT PROJECT AMONG MEDICAL IMAGING, LUTHERAN HOSPITAL, AND VERA BRADLEY DESIGNS, THE WOMEN'S CANCER CENTER HAS BEEN DESIGNED AS A SAFE HAVEN FOR WOMEN DIAGNOSED WITH CANCER.

AS STAFF MEMBERS AT MEDICAL IMAGING WORK TO FACILITATE CHANGE IN THE MEDICAL INDUSTRY, THEY REALIZE THAT MEDICAL ATTENTION ALSO MEANS COMPASSION AND CARE.

MEDICAL IMAGING PROVIDES RAPID RESULTS, WITH A TURNAROUND TIME OF 24 HOURS OR LESS. AN ONSITE RADIOLOGIST IS READILY AVAILABLE TO ANSWER PATIENTS' QUESTIONS.

medical industry, the staff realizes that medical attention also means compassion and care. Not only is there extensive interaction between the patients and radiologists at Medical Imaging, there's also a great deal of care and attention to the emotional needs of patients. For example, to ease the anxiety of women obtaining mammography screenings, Medical Imaging offers a private reception area complete with books, beverages, television, comfortable furnishings, and peace and quiet. In 1998, Medical Imaging extended its most outward sign of care to patients by collaborating on the Women's Cancer Center.

The first of its kind in Indiana, the Women's Cancer Center at Lutheran Hospital is a joint project among Medical Imaging, Lutheran Hospital, and Vera Bradley Designs. The center has been designed as a safe haven for women diagnosed with cancer, and is decorated in a manner that sets it apart from other clinical settings. Unique fabrics, colors, and furniture are used to create a nurturing, homelike atmosphere. Yellow is the primary decorating color, symbolizing hope and optimism. The interior design and furnishings were all created by Vera Bradley Designs. The center is a place where women talk and

receive more information about cancer through access to a library of books and brochures, the Internet, and support groups that meet regularly at the center. In addition, spouses and families of women with cancer use the center to help relieve their fears and concerns. Since its opening in 1998, the center has cared for the needs of hundreds of women every month.

As part of its desire to speed discovery of a cure for cancer, Medical Imaging sponsors the Vera Bradley Classic, an annual women's tennis and golf event that raises money for breast cancer research. Medical Imaging also offers for sale a book *Just Peachy: Cooking Up a Cure for*

Cancer. Proceeds from the cookbook—which features recipes from people including President Bill Clinton, Senator Richard Lugar, and many Indiana state officials, professors, and residents—support breast cancer research at the Indiana University Cancer Center.

In the next millennium, Medical Imaging will continue to bring quality care to patients in and around the Northeast Indiana region, at the same time facing everyday challenges as technology evolves and Medical Imaging expands its network of providers and locations. Yet its focus will always be on the human element as it works to meet the physical and emotional needs of each and every patient.

DESIGN COLLABORATIVE

FOR ARCHITECTS AND ENGINEERS, A GREAT REPUTATION— and the quality projects that come with it—is achieved after a lifetime of work and commitment. For Design Collaborative, this status has arrived ahead of schedule. This young architecture/engineering firm has built a reputation for facilitative problem solving, comprehensive services, and innovative solutions that respond to the unique opportunities and limitations of the company's clients. The result is an impressive array of projects receiving local and national recognition.

Located in Fort Wayne's historic Farmers Market Plaza, Design Collaborative was established in 1992. As its name suggests, the firm promotes the building design process as a team effort. Founded on the principle that clients should be active members of the project team, Design Collaborative believes client involvement provides valuable insight into projects. As a result, satisfied customers are the norm for the firm—80 percent of its workload comes from repeat clients.

EXPERTISE IN HIGHER EDUCATION

Colleges and universities throughout the Midwest form a significant part of Design Collaborative's work. Its master planning services aid institutions in identifying and developing their visions. With projects ranging from residence halls and recreation centers to classroom buildings and information centers, the firm provides clients with a strong background of experience, including expertise in technology integration, which allows clients to make accommodations for their ever evolving needs in new and existing facilities.

Locally, Design Collaborative has played an important role in the growth at the University of Saint Francis. Recent projects include the new Doermer Family Center for Health Sciences and the Mimi and Ian Rolland Art and Visual Communication Center. In addition, the new football stadium provides an added home-field advantage for the NCAA Division II Cougars.

A striking example of Design Collaborative's work is the award-winning Indiana Wesleyan University's Music and Performing Arts Center in Marion. The 1,150-seat auditorium also features a 180-seat recital hall, a black-box rehearsal theater, practice rooms, classrooms, and faculty offices. Other major projects include the university's Adult and Professional Studies Building, wellness and recreation center, and science building, as well as its upcoming library/information center.

DIVERSE CORPORATE CLIENTS

Design Collaborative continues to develop a strong reputation with corporate clients. The firm's nationally recognized clients include such Fort Wayne-based firms as Lincoln National Corporation, Navistar, Bank One, Raytheon, GTE, and NIPSCO, as well as such regionally based firms as Parke-Davis, Owens Corning, and Corporate Family Solutions. But local firms continue to be an important part of the Design's Collaborative workload as well. "These are companies— often with unique needs and desires—that directly impact the local fabric and quality of life," says President Pat Pasterick.

Fort Wayne-based Brotherhood Mutual Insurance's expansion plans included updating the image of the company's existing corporate headquarters and making accommodations for technol-

THE INDIANA WESLEYAN UNIVERSITY MUSIC AND PERFORMING ARTS CENTER, DESIGNED BY DESIGN COLLABORATIVE, IS HOME TO NATIONALLY RECOGNIZED CHORAL AND INSTRUMENTAL PROGRAMS, AS WELL AS TO A GROWING THEATER PROGRAM.

ogy. Design Collaborative's solution was a state-of-the-art addition and strategic modifications to the existing facility. The result is a unified facility that is extremely flexible and provides a simple, elegant, high-tech image.

The Tuthill Corporation, Fillrite Division, located in an industrial park near the Fort Wayne International Airport, is an example of a project with an owner dedicated to expressing a corporate philosophy through building design. Design Collaborative's building design reinforces the client's desire for openness, and creates a strong connection between administrative and manufacturing processes. The design strengthens the owner's ability to encourage pride in the workplace.

NEAL BRUNS

COMMITMENT TO CLIENTS

Design Collaborative's success, Pasterick believes, is due in large part to the commitment the firm provides to clients. "Our approach to design is to involve the client as a teammate," says Pasterick. "Together, we develop an overlap of vision and commitment, not only to the project, but to each other. We strive not just to meet their expectations, but to exceed them." Clients work with a team of architects and engineers who stay with the project from the earliest programming phases until the final interior finishes are applied. Aiming for complete client satisfaction, each team works to create unique designs while working within predetermined construction budgets. Service extends to utilizing a variety of forms of communication—verbal, graphic, and three-dimensional computer modeling—to aid clients in visualizing the many phases of project development.

Design Collaborative is also committed to excellence in design, which is reflected by awards the company has received from the American Institute of Architects and American School and University magazine, among others. "Excellence in design means more than how good a facility looks," says Pasterick. "It involves how well the building works for the users and how it fits with its surroundings. We don't design

DESIGN COLLABORATIVE'S BUILDING DESIGN FOR TUTHILL CORPORATION'S OFFICES AND MANUFACTURING FACILITY, LOCATED NEAR THE FORT WAYNE INTERNATIONAL AIRPORT, REINFORCES THE CLIENT'S DESIRE FOR OPENNESS, AND CREATES A STRONG CONNECTION BETWEEN ADMINISTRATIVE AND MANUFACTURING PROCESSES.

DESIGN COLLABORATIVE CONVERTED A UNIQUE, EIGHT-STORY OFFICE BUILDING AND PARKING GARAGE INTO THE LINCOLN LIFE TRAINING CENTER, WHICH SERVES 5,000 EMPLOYEES IN FORT WAYNE.

buildings to win awards; we design them to meet needs. The way clients interact with our teams has led to opportunities to meet those needs in creative ways."

BECOMING THE BEST

Design Collaborative looks to the future with a bright eye and a commitment to the city. As a Fort Wayne firm, the company is dedicated to clients in the surrounding area. "This is where our families and friends are, and

there is a great deal of satisfaction in working with clients to realize their dreams and to have a positive influence in the community," says Pasterick. He also sees the firm growing in other regions of the country as its reputation continues to expand.

However, growth is not Design Collaborative's prime concern. "We've never wanted to be the biggest firm," Pasterick continues. "We think it's more important to strive to be the best."

Steel Dynamics, Inc.

Over a beer in downtown Indianapolis in the summer of 1993, Fort Wayne native Keith Busse called for a vote. "I'll never forget that moment," he says. "We banged our glasses together and decided to go for it. We decided to take advantage of our skills and proceed with the adventure of our lifetimes."

The "we" who met together in Indianapolis were Busse, Mark Millett, and Dick Teets, all Nucor Corporation managers who had built the company's Crawfordsville, Indiana, steel mill, where, with great success, they had pioneered a new steelmaking technology called continuous thin-slab casting. Celebrated both within the industry and in the popular press for virtually revolutionizing American steelmaking, the three had nonetheless been passed over for promotions at Nucor, and all were ready for a new challenge.

The three men's new adventure, proposed in the summer of 1993, was the formation of Steel Dynamics, Inc. (SDI), the first new, unaffiliated greenfield American steelmaker without preexisting financial credentials to be created in more than 100 years—and for good reason. Big Steel began to decline in the early 1970s and had almost perished by the early 1980s, having for too long failed to keep its capital, material, labor, and energy costs in check, and having let its market share erode in the face of offshore competition.

"Nucor's mini mill at Crawfordsville helped America become prominent and competitive again

in the world steelmaking community, as opposed to being the laughingstock of the world," Busse says. And he, Teets, and Millett were determined to take mini-mill technology to the next level.

The Revolution Continued

Based on the trio's Nucor success, investors sunk $370 million into the privately held SDI, which chose to locate its new mill in northeastern Indiana, between Big Steel and one of Big Steel's biggest customers, the automotive industry. The facility—near Butler, east of Auburn—was up and running in 14 months, a new

world record, and was producing high-quality steel at a record low cost, competing with Big Steel for customers.

What the partners had pioneered at Crawfordsville was further refined at Butler. They helped pioneer technology modifications that could cast steel even faster and roll it even thinner than ever before. They shortcut the archaic and expensive manufacturing process Big Steel used to make sheet steel. SDI's state-of-the-art thin-slab-casting equipment and control technologies, low capital costs, relatively low energy use, and environmental

CLOCKWISE FROM TOP: IN 1993, DICK TEETS, KEITH BUSSE, AND MARK MILLETT—ALL FORMER NUCOR CORPORATION EMPLOYEES—FORMED STEEL DYNAMICS, INC. (SDI). SHORTLY AFTER THE COMPANY'S FOUNDING, TRACY SHELLABARGER (RIGHT), ALSO A FORMER NUCOR EMPLOYEE, JOINED SDI AS ITS CHIEF FINANCIAL OFFICER.

MORE THAN 1 MILLION SQUARE FEET ARE UNDER ROOF AT SDI'S BUTLER, INDIANA, FACILITY, WHICH HOUSES THE HOT MILL, COLD MILL, AND ITS WHOLLY OWNED SUBSIDIARY, IRON DYNAMICS.

AN OPERATOR MONITORS A FLOW OF MOLTEN PIG IRON TAPPED FROM IRON DYNAMICS' SUBMERGED-ARC FURNACE.

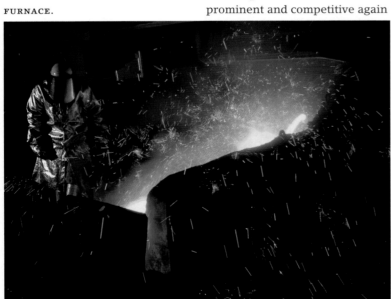

friendliness set world records. So did the company's low-cost production. Whereas Big Steel spent three to four hours making a ton of prime steel, SDI's thin-slab mill produces a ton in 20 to 25 minutes.

SDI has become one of the most profitable companies in the steelmaking community, showing consistent profitability following its start-up year. Its Flat Roll Steel Division leads American steel producers in its operating profit per ton. And the division has accomplished this goal while maintaining an excellent environmental record.

What's more, the company has developed a strong reputation as a quality leader, supplying a broad range of flat-rolled steel products to American industry, including light-gauge, micro-alloyed, and high-strength steels. A growing percentage of SDI's output is used in exacting automotive applications. The company also has been an industry leader in the use of the Internet for commercial transactions. Best of all, SDI's order book has been full from the start.

An Economic Boon

Investors have been impressed. A public stock offering in the fall of 1996 raised $140 million, which allowed SDI to expand its operation, becoming a full-line steel producer able to compete with Big Steel for lucrative business. A second public stock offering in 1997 raised $30 million.

Since its founding, SDI has been in a constant state of expansion. It has doubled its hot-mill casting capacity at the Butler mill, and added a cold-mill operation, which permits the company to

produce thinner-gauge steel and to apply various coatings and other treatments to its own product—resulting in value-added steel for its customers and increased profits for SDI. A wholly owned subsidiary, Iron Dynamics, converts iron ore into pig iron, thus providing a low-cost substitute for scrap steel. SDI plans to construct a second mini mill—this one to make structural steel and rail. The company has also invested in a building-products subsidiary, New Millennium Building Systems. New Millennium manufactures steel joists, trusses, and girders, as well as roof and floor decking for use in nonresidential construction. And SDI has constructed a new headquarters southwest of Fort Wayne.

Busse and his partners have been an economic boon to northeastern Indiana. They have brought exceptional opportunities to their nearly 700 employees, a number that will grow to about 1,000 with the completion of the structural-steel and rail mill. At SDI, steelworkers make an excellent living while being part of a promising new venture. Their extraordinary incentives include high base pay, stock options, profit sharing, and performance bonuses tied to productivity, quality, and cost reduction.

"We believe the top-notch, talented individuals we have attracted are second to none," Busse says. "They allow SDI to maximize the effectiveness of modern steelmaking technologies."

CLOCKWISE FROM TOP: A STEEL COIL, FRESH FROM AN SDI COLD MILL'S GALVANIZING LINE, IS PREPARED FOR SHIPMENT.

A COLD MILL OPERATOR WELDS THE TAIL END OF A STEEL COIL TO THE HEAD END OF THE NEXT COIL TO BE PROCESSED, PROVIDING CONTINUOUS MATERIAL FLOW THROUGHOUT THE GALVANIZING OPERATION.

A GLOWING SLAB OF STEEL—AT 1,650 DEGREES FAHRENHEIT—ROLLS FROM A THIN-SLAB CASTER IN SDI'S FLAT-ROLL STEEL MILL.

COVINGTON COMMONS SENIOR COMMUNITY

A unique organization, Covington Commons Senior Community fosters independence and promotes a high quality of life for its residents. That focus is at the forefront of its efforts to become the premier senior community in the Fort Wayne area. ◆ "When people think of senior living, I want them to think of Covington Commons," says General Manager Susan Myers. "By providing whatever services residents need, we keep their levels of independence as high as possible for as long as possible."

BRINGING HOME AND HEALTH TOGETHER

Covington Commons is part of American Senior Communities, an Indianapolis-based firm that owns and operates similar senior communities throughout the state of Indiana. American Senior Communities provides a variety of lifestyle choices and services, so that as residents' needs change, they can stay within the community they have come to trust and enjoy.

Covington Commons offers one- and two-bedroom Garden Homes, each with a year-round sunroom, garage, and appliances. Garden Home residents enjoy maintenance-free living with access to community services such as meals, housekeeping, transportation, and activities. Assisted Living residents can choose from three different floor plans. Rent includes meals in the Orchard Café, housekeeping, all utilities except telephone, scheduled trans-portation, and planned social and recreational activities. Both Garden Home and Assisted Living apartments include a 24-hour emergency response system. In case of emergency, residents press a pendant they keep with them or a button in the bathroom, and a message is delivered to the in-house home health staff.

The location of Covington Commons was strategically planned by American Senior Communities. The community is situated within 10 minutes of Lutheran Hospital and less than five minutes from dozens of shopping venues, restaurants, and banks. "For a senior who can still drive but doesn't want to go far for services, Covington Commons is ideal," says Director of Sales Eric N. Langlois.

Part of Covington Commons' uniqueness stems from its philosophy that residents are individuals and should be treated as such. The staff of Covington Commons tailors care to the needs of each resident. For example, although assisted living services usually encompass assistance with dressing, bathing, and taking medications, Covington Commons provides only the care a resident needs or desires. If that means assistance only in dressing, then the resident pays only for that service. The resident can always decrease or increase the level of care as needed. This arrangement is particularly beneficial for residents who are recovering from an illness or injury and need care on a temporary basis.

COMMUNITY WITHIN A COMMUNITY

As part of its desire to foster independence and create a community setting, Covington Commons offers many in-house services. It sponsors weekly wellness programs run by American Senior Home Care, whose staff provides the home health care services at Covington Commons. Residents can also take advantage of beauty, podiatry, and hearing aid services, along with an in-house general store for the convenience of the residents.

The Orchard Café features an open-dining plan with restaurant-style service. Residents are free to sit where they like, they can place their order with the dining room staff from a menu that changes daily, and the staff serves

COVINGTON COMMONS SENIOR COMMUNITY SPONSORS WEEKLY WELLNESS PROGRAMS RUN BY AMERICAN SENIOR HOME CARE, WHOSE STAFF PROVIDES HOME HEALTH CARE SERVICES TO THE COMMUNITY'S RESIDENTS.

the resident. The Orchard Café also hosts special dinners. Each month, it holds a special birthday buffet for all residents who are celebrating birthdays that month. And on Valentine's Day, Covington Commons sponsors the annual Sweetheart Ball with a special meal complete with dancing and the crowning of the king and queen.

Worship opportunities are another important aspect of Covington Commons' amenities. Services are held for members of various faiths, including Catholic, Baptist, Lutheran, Methodist, and nondenominational residents. A chapel is available for meditation, prayer gatherings, and communion.

Activities are also a favorite of residents of the community. Topping the list is Energy Exercise, which meets three times a week, along with Looking Back, Team Trivia, and Interesting Inspirations. In addition, residents enjoy outings hosted by the community. Covington Commons chauffeurs residents to shopping malls, grocery stores, doctors' offices, and special places like Bearcreek Farms, the Lincoln Museum, and the Fort Wayne Children's Zoo.

COMMUNITY INVOLVEMENT

Part of Myers' job involves educating the community about assisted living. "Most people don't understand assisted living or what we offer," she says. "They think we're a nursing home or we don't have enough care to provide residents what they need. Neither is true. We offer choice to Fort Wayne seniors."

To increase awareness about the community's programs, Myers speaks with doctors, social workers, and various organizations about the larger role Covington Commons is playing in the Fort Wayne area. Covington Commons has been involved in the Over-50 Sock Hop, an event held during the Three Rivers Festival. It is also one of the sponsors for the Vera Bradley Classic, which raises money for breast cancer research. In addition, the residents of Covington Commons have organized Cards of Loving Kindness, where they recycle greeting cards for resale and donate the proceeds to a local charity. All of these activities reflect Covington Commons' guiding principle: to provide a community where residents thrive in all aspects of life.

"Covington Commons is home to our residents," Myers says. "From the minute you walk in the door, you feel the warm, caring atmosphere. Our residents have the best of both worlds here: a place where they can be cared for if needed, but at the same time, where they can maintain their independence in their own space. We often hear our residents say, 'I should have done this sooner.'"

THE ORCHARD CAFÉ AT COVINGTON COMMONS FEATURES AN OPEN-DINING PLAN WITH RESTAURANT-STYLE SERVICE. RESIDENTS ARE FREE TO SIT WHERE THEY LIKE, AND THEY CAN PLACE THEIR ORDER WITH THE DINING ROOM STAFF FROM A MENU THAT CHANGES DAILY.

PART OF COVINGTON COMMONS UNIQUENESS STEMS FROM ITS PHILOSOPHY THAT RESIDENTS ARE INDIVIDUALS AND SHOULD BE TREATED AS SUCH.

Budget Rent a Car of Fort Wayne

VEHICLE RENTAL PLAYS A SURPRISINGLY LARGE ROLE IN the makeup of the American economy. In 1997, the car rental industry in the United States generated more than $16 billion in revenues. That same year, there were more than 1.6 million cars available to rent at more than 21,000 U.S. locations. ◆ Budget Rent a Car of Fort Wayne is part of that booming industry. Originally located downtown, Budget moved to Fort Wayne International Airport in the late 1980s, and in 1998, the company opened another Budget Rent a Car in the Budget Car sales facility on Lima Road. These Fort Wayne locations report to regional offices in Indianapolis.

CORPORATE CLIENTS DRIVE GROWTH

With estimated worldwide revenues in 1997 of $2.7 billion, the Budget System employs approximately 24,500 people in more than 3,200 locations. Budget's Fort Wayne locations employ some 20 people.

Following national trends in car rental, corporate clients who are flying in and out of Fort Wayne International Airport make up 60 percent of Budget's clients. The remaining 40 percent consists of Fort Wayne residents who are renting cars for vacations or as replacement cars while theirs are being fixed.

Business from corporate clients remains consistent throughout the year, yet local business is seasonable. "We've been able to count on consistent need from corporate clients to fuel our growth," says Budget City Manager Andy Klein.

SPECIALIZED VEHICLES

Budget's variety of vehicles is one feature that sets it apart from its competition—currently, the company has one of the largest specialty rental fleets in the world, ranging from sport utility vehicles to convertibles. In 1998, Budget's fleet in the United States averaged 131,000 vehicles, and its fleet worldwide totaled 265,000 vehicles.

In Fort Wayne, the company rents everything from standard vehicles to full-sized four-wheel drives to passenger vans. Budget's 15 vans are popular with schools and church groups. Another one of the company's specialties in Fort Wayne is cargo trucks. Budget offers 15 cargo trucks for one or two-way rentals. "That's a market niche we have filled," says Klein.

In the future, Budget hopes to continue to expand the size of its fleet and to increase the number of its locations in Fort Wayne. The company plans to open at least two more locations around Fort Wayne in the next few years, and will determine those locations by observing the city's population trends. Explains Klein, "We'll track where people are living and serve those areas."

Successfully meeting the needs of its customers through convenient locations and a wide variety of vehicle options, Budget is sure to continue serving the Fort Wayne area for many years to come.

◆ JONATHAN POSTAL

◆ JONATHAN POSTAL

BUDGET RENT A CAR OF FORT WAYNE RENTS CARS, TRUCKS, AND VANS TO BUSINESS TRAVELERS AND VACATIONERS ALIKE.

TOWERY PUBLISHING, INC.

BEGINNING AS A SMALL PUBLISHER OF LOCAL NEWSpapers in the 1930s, Towery Publishing, Inc. today produces a wide range of community-oriented materials, including books (Urban Tapestry Series), business directories, magazines, and Internet publications. Building on its long heritage of excellence, the company has become global in scope, with cities from San Diego to Sydney represented by Towery products. In all its endeavors, this Memphis-based company strives to be synonymous with service, utility, and quality.

A DIVERSITY OF COMMUNITY-BASED PRODUCTS

Over the years, Towery has become the largest producer of published materials for North American chambers of commerce. From membership directories that enhance business-to-business communication to visitor and relocation guides tailored to reflect the unique qualities of the communities they cover, the company's chamber-oriented materials offer comprehensive information on dozens of topics, including housing, education, leisure activities, health care, and local government.

In 1998, the company acquired Cincinnati-based Target Marketing, an established provider of detailed city street maps to more than 200 chambers of commerce throughout the United States and Canada. Now a division of Towery, Target offers full-color maps that include local landmarks and points of interest, such as recreational parks, shopping centers, golf courses, schools, industrial parks, city and county limits, subdivision names, public buildings, and even block numbers on most streets.

In 1990, Towery launched the Urban Tapestry Series, an award-winning collection of oversized, hardbound photojournals detailing the people, history, culture, environment, and commerce of various metropolitan areas. These coffee-table books highlight a community through three basic elements: an introductory essay by a noted local individual, an exquisite collection of four-color photographs, and profiles of the companies and organizations that animate the area's business life.

To date, more than 80 Urban Tapestry Series editions have been published in cities around the world, from New York to Vancouver to Sydney. Authors of the books' introductory essays include former U.S. President Gerald Ford (Grand Rapids), former Alberta Premier Peter Lougheed (Calgary), CBS anchor Dan Rather (Austin), ABC anchor Hugh Downs (Phoenix), bestselling mystery author Robert B. Parker (Boston), American Movie Classics host Nick Clooney (Cincinnati), Senator Richard Lugar (Indianapolis), and Challenger Center founder June Scobee Rodgers (Chattanooga).

To maintain hands-on quality in all of its periodicals and books, Towery has long used the latest production methods available. The company was the first production environment in the United States to combine desktop publishing with color separations and image scanning to produce finished film suitable for burning plates for four-color printing. Today, Towery relies on state-of-the-art digital prepress services to produce more than 8,000 pages each year, containing more than 30,000 high-quality color images.

AN INTERNET PIONEER

By combining its long-standing expertise in community-oriented published materials with advanced production capabilities, a global sales force, and extensive data management capabilities, Towery has emerged as a significant provider of Internet-based city

TOWERY PUBLISHING PRESIDENT AND CEO J. ROBERT TOWERY HAS EXPANDED THE BUSINESS HIS PARENTS STARTED IN THE 1930S TO INCLUDE A GROWING ARRAY OF TRADITIONAL AND ELECTRONIC PUBLISHED MATERIALS, AS WELL AS INTERNET AND MULTIMEDIA SERVICES, THAT ARE MARKETED LOCALLY, NATIONALLY, AND INTERNATIONALLY.

STEVE DAVIS

information. In keeping with its overall focus on community resources, the company's Internet efforts represent a natural step in the evolution of the business.

The primary product lines within the Internet division are the introCity™ sites. Towery's introCity sites introduce newcomers, visitors, and longtime residents to every facet of a particular community, while simultaneously placing the local chamber of commerce at the forefront of the city's Internet activity. The sites include newcomer information, calendars, photos, citywide business listings with everything from nightlife to shopping to family fun, and on-line maps pinpointing the exact location of businesses, schools, attractions, and much more.

DECADES OF PUBLISHING EXPERTISE

In 1972, current President and CEO J. Robert Towery succeeded his parents in managing the printing and publishing business they had founded nearly four decades earlier. Soon thereafter, he expanded the scope of the company's published materials to include Memphis magazine and other successful regional and national publications. In 1985, after sell-

ing its locally focused assets, Towery began the trajectory on which it continues today, creating community-oriented materials that are often produced in

conjunction with chambers of commerce and other business organizations.

Despite the decades of change, Towery himself follows a long-standing family philosophy of unmatched service and unflinching quality. That approach extends throughout the entire organization to include more than 120 employees at the Memphis headquarters, another 80 located in Northern Kentucky outside Cincinnati, and more than 40 sales, marketing, and editorial staff traveling to and working in a growing list of client cities. All of its products, and more information about the company, are featured on the Internet at www.towery.com.

In summing up his company's steady growth, Towery restates the essential formula that has driven the business since its first pages were published: "The creative energies of our staff drive us toward innovation and invention. Our people make the highest possible demands on themselves, so I know that our future is secure if the ingredients for success remain a focus on service and

TOWERY PUBLISHING WAS THE FIRST PRODUCTION ENVIRONMENT IN THE UNITED STATES TO COMBINE DESKTOP PUBLISHING WITH COLOR SEPARATIONS AND IMAGE SCANNING TO PRODUCE FINISHED FILM SUITABLE FOR BURNING PLATES FOR FOUR-COLOR PRINTING. TODAY, THE COMPANY'S STATE-OF-THE-ART NETWORK OF MACINTOSH AND WINDOWS WORKSTATIONS ALLOWS IT TO PRODUCE MORE THAN 8,000 PAGES EACH YEAR, CONTAINING MORE THAN 30,000 HIGH-QUALITY COLOR IMAGES (TOP).

THE TOWERY FAMILY'S PUBLISHING ROOTS CAN BE TRACED TO 1935, WHEN R.W. TOWERY (FAR LEFT) BEGAN PRODUCING A SERIES OF COMMUNITY HISTORIES IN TENNESSEE, MISSISSIPPI, AND TEXAS. THROUGHOUT THE COMPANY'S HISTORY, THE FOUNDING FAMILY HAS CONSISTENTLY EXHIBITED A COMMITMENT TO CLARITY, PRECISION, INNOVATION, AND VISION (BOTTOM).

PHOTOGRAPHERS

STEVE BAKER began working with Highlight Photography while attending Indiana University, and, since then, has contributed to more than 200 publications, including a number of Urban Tapestry books. His corporate clients include Eastman Kodak, Mobil Oil, the U.S. Olympic Committee, and Budweiser, and he owns a library of more than 50,000 marketable images from his travels across the country.

© BILL CHRISTIE

Originally from Fort Wayne, THOMAS L. BOSSERMAN is a member of the Fort Wayne Photography Club and is a co-owner of locally based Cole Research and Development. A Vietnam veteran, he is involved in several community projects and has a patent currently pending for a new chemical process/product.

Armed with degrees in both fine arts and business administration, BILL CHRISTIE currently works for Sunny Schick Camera Shop and specializes in special effects and black-and-white photography. A Chicago native, he has won numerous awards from competitions in Indiana and Ohio.

Specializing in child, animal, and sports photography, CHERYL A. ERTELT has had images in more than 70 publications, including photographs in USA Today and Sporting News. Originally from Indianapolis, she has participated in two photo safaris in Kenya.

LARRY S. FISHER began photographing fires as a hobby in 1981. A native of Fort Wayne, he works for the Fort Wayne Fire Department and has been published in Firehouse magazine, Hot Shots, and other regional publications.

JUDITH GAULDEN contributes regularly to the local arts community with publications in the Here's Fort Wayne calendar and displays at the Fort Wayne Museum of Art. Working at Photo Artistry by Judy, she specializes in wedding photography and portraiture.

Working through a stock agency, LYNN GERIG takes most of his photographs while hiking and backpacking in the western mountain states and provinces of North America. He is originally from rural Allen County and specializes in nature photography.

Associated with two stock photo agencies, SHARON GERIG specializes in nature photography. She has been published in an assortment of textbooks, calendars, advertisements, and other publications, and is a life-long resident of Allen County.

Self-employed since 1994, PALERMO G. GALINDO won Best of College Photography at Indiana University in 2000 after placing as a finalist in 1997 and 1998. His clients include Minnesota Life Insurance, Fort Wayne's Business People Magazine, and KMC Telecom. With degrees in commercial art and graphic design, Galindo specializes in black-and-white infrared art and color photography of skylines, weddings, and corporate and environmental portraits.

Originally from the Northeast, MARV GOTTLIEB does contract work for Golfpix/Multipix and is a senior staff photographer for several Fort Wayne publications. A frequent contributor to Business People Magazine, he is a member of the National Press Photographers Association, Chicago Broadcast Advertising Club, and Fort Wayne Advertising Federation.

In 1990, CATHLEEN L. HUFF cofounded Written on the Wind, a communications consulting company that specializes in the research and presentation of photography. Originally from the Fort Wayne area, she works in a variety of photography specialties.

Originally from New York, GARY INGLESE received his MBA from Indiana Wesleyan and is a resident of Fort Wayne.

BILL KERCHEVAL is the former production photographer for the Indiana University Purdue University, Fort Wayne Theatre Department. He has received several honorable mention awards and acceptance to a number of area photography contests and displays, including the Honeywell 100 in Wabash, Indiana, and the Van Wert Art Contest in Van Wert, Ohio. Kercheval has had several pieces loaned to the Fort Wayne Museum of Art, and has been published in the U.S. Naval Institute's publication Proceedings.

MARC A. LANSKY has been the recipient of a number of honors in several national and international contests, including an International Newspaper Snapshot Award and an Editor's Choice award from the Library of Photography. He supplies images to several businesses and business publications, including the *Here's Fort Wayne* calendar, and teaches photography for Indiana University Purdue University, Fort Wayne adult education classes.

BUD LEE studied at the Columbia University School of Fine Arts in New York and the National Academy of Fine Arts before moving to the Orlando area more than 20 years ago. A self-employed photojournalist, he founded the Florida Photographers Workshop and the Iowa Photographers Workshop. Lee's work can be seen in *Esquire, Life, Travel & Leisure, Rolling Stone,* the *Washington Post,* and the *New York Times,* as well as in several Urban Tapestry Series publications.

As a freelance photographer, JOHN MERZ has been awarded numerous honors for excellence in photography. Specializing in architecture, landscape, travel, and nature photography, he has been published in the *Here's Fort Wayne* calendar and the Fort Wayne Annual Report.

NICK T. NICHOLAS is a freelance photographer specializing in zoological and commercial photography. He has done extensive work for the Fort Wayne Children's Zoo and numerous local corporations. A veteran of African safaris and expeditions to Antarctica, he has field experience on all seven continents. His images have been presented as gifts to the United States Air Force Thunderbirds; the city officials of Takaoka, Japan; and several Australian dignitaries.

Originally from Cleveland, TOM NITZA has been photographing in Fort Wayne for more than 25 years.

JUDI PARKS is an award-winning photojournalist working from the San Francisco Bay Area. Her work

appears in numerous museums and public collections in the United States and Europe. Her documentary series *Home Sweet Home: Caring for America's Elderly* was recently honored with the Communication Arts-Design Annual 1999 Award of Excellence for an unpublished series.

SUZANNE J. ROGERS entered the world of professional photography when she started her own business, Q Cards, and photographed a number of local landmarks. Working mostly in black and white, she works with 10 retail businesses in Fort Wayne and has shown her work at the Fort Wayne Museum of Art and the Honeywell Center.

Specializing in large-format photography, DR. LOUIS F. ROMAIN has had his work judged and accepted for exhibition in more than 2,600 sanctioned international photographic salons in 76 countries. He is active in photoeducation and has published numerous articles about diverse aspects of photography. In addition, he has been published in several *Here's Fort Wayne* calendars.

As a past president of the Fort Wayne Photographers Club, JIM TRAINER specializes in monochrome prints. He has studied in Fort Wayne and has received numerous photography awards from area newspapers.

Originally from South Dakota, DONALD J. VOELKER specializes in freelance landscape photography and has had photographs published in coffee-table books, magazines, and calendars. He manages his own Web page and business, and enjoys photographing old mills, covered bridges, and barns.

Additional photographers and organizations that contributed to *Fort Wayne: City of Spirit* include the African-American Museum, Auburn

Cord Duesenberg Museum, Embassy Centre, Fort Wayne Komets, Fort Wayne Wizards, Galliher Studios, Eldon Horner, Joe Taylor and the Redbirds, the *Journal Gazette,* and Parkview Hospital. Please contact Towery Publishing for additional information about photographers with images in *Fort Wayne: City of Spirit.*

LIBRARY OF CONGRESS CATALOGING-IN-PUBLICATION DATA

Edwards, Keith, 1952-
    Fort Wayne : city of spirit / by Keith Edwards ; art direction by Brian Groppe.
      p.   cm. — (Urban tapestry series)
    Includes index.
    ISBN 1-881096-75-0 (alk. paper)
    1. Fort Wayne (Ind.)—Civilization. 2. Fort Wayne (Ind.)—Pictorial works. 3. Fort Wayne (Ind.)—Economic conditions. 4. Business enterprises—Indiana—Fort Wayne. I. Title. II. Series.

F534.F7 E35 2000
977.2'74—dc21
                                          00-047984

Towery Publishing, Inc.
The Towery Building
1835 Union Avenue
Memphis, TN 38104

WWW.TOWERY.COM

Publisher: J. Robert Towery **Executive Publisher**: Jenny McDowell **National Sales Manager**: Stephen Hung **Marketing Director**: Carol Culpepper **Project Directors**: Lisa Enlow Black, Mary Hanley, Henry Hintermeister **Executive Editor**: David B. Dawson **Managing Editor**: Lynn Conlee **Senior Editors**: Carlisle Hacker, Brian L. Johnston **Editor/Profile Manager**: Stephen M. Deusner **Editors**: Jay Adkins, Rebecca E. Farabough, Ginny Reeves, Sabrina Schroeder **Copy Editor**: Danna M. Greenfield **Profile Writer**: Karen Asp **Caption Writer**: Stephen M. Deusner **Photography Editor**: Jonathan Postal **Photographic Consultant**: James M. Schmelzer **Profile Designers**: Rebekah Barnhardt, Laurie Beck, Glen Marshall **Production Manager**: Brenda Pattat **Photography Coordinator**: Robin Lankford **Production Assistants**: Robert Barnett, Loretta Lane **Digital Color Supervisor**: Darin Ipema **Digital Color Technicians**: Eric Friedl, Brent Salazar **Color Scanning Technicians**: Brad Long, Mark Svetz **Production Resources Manager**: Dave Dunlap Jr. **Print Coordinator**: Beverly Timmons

INDEX TO PROFILES

© JUDI PARKS